being the bird

poems and prayers
new and selected
mary wickham

First Published in Australia in 2021
by Spectrum Publications Pty Ltd
a: PO Box 75, Richmond, Vic. 3121
t: (+61) 1300 540 376
f: (+61) 1300 540 737
spectrum@spectrumpublications.com.au
www.spectrumpublications.com.au
for Mary Wickham
www.marywickhamrsm.org.au

Copyright 2021 Institute Property Association Limited of the Institute of the Sisters of Mercy of Australia and Papua New Guinea.
All rights reserved. No part of this publication may be reproduced in any manner without prior written permission of the publisher.

Cover image by Rene Magritte, Untitled.

ISBN 978 0 86786 080-1

In loving memory of
my parents
~ Stella Kathleen Cannon and Philip Simon Wickham ~
and my Sisters in Mercy
~ Sr Patricia Kenny ~
and
~ Sr Clare Conway ~

After the timber has been sawn
Rough rings release the song of the place-
Droughts, good summers, long frosts-
The way pain and joy unlock in a voice.

                                                         Moya Cannon

We can make our minds so like still water
that beings gather about us
that they may see,
it may be, their own images,
and live for a moment with a clearer,
perhaps even with a fiercer life because of our quiet.

                                                         W B Yeats

This huge trusted power
Is spirit (which) moves in the muscle of the world,
In continual creation.

                                                Elizabeth Jennings

acknowledgements

This collection includes a large number of previously unpublished poems, as well as poems published on my website http://marywickhamrsm.org.au and my two previous collections, *In The Water Was The Fire* and *Souvenirs of Spirit*. It also reprints a number of prayers and blessings related to Mercy, some of which were commissioned by Mercy International Centre, Dublin.

Several of the poems were shortlisted for the Australian Catholic University Poetry Prize and published in the respective chapbooks: *Dance of the Seagulls* (2016) *Rosslare Ferry* (2018) *Islands* (2019) and *Kite At Williamstown* (2020)

The poem *The Four Hundred* won the Max Harris Poetry Award. A number of poems were originally published in magazines in the USA, Ireland and Australia.

I thank Sr Eveline Crotty and the Leadership Team of The Institute of Sisters of Mercy of Australia and Papua New Guinea for their generous funding of this publication.

I am grateful to Peter Rohr and all at Spectrum Publications, for their expertise, commitment and care, and I acknowledge particularly Maria Rohr who graciously published my first collection in 1995.

The Introduction to my first collection *In The Water Was the Fire*, written by Michael Leunig, is reprinted in this collection. I remain grateful to Michael for his generous reading of those earlier poems, some of which are reprinted in this book.

Thanks to the Wickham, Cannon and Uccellini families for their encouragement, support and inspiration, and for tolerating the occasional touch of poetic licence.

contents

Kite At Williamstown	1
Covid-19 Haiku	2
Wonder	3
Starling	4
Jewel	5
Dance of the Seagulls	6
Amen	8
Gallarus 1	10
Gallarus 2	11
Islands	12
Callanish Perspective	14
Bird in the Hand	16
Word on a Wall	18
Only The Best	19
The Etymology of Relief	20
Rosslare Ferry	22
Questing	24
How	25
Real Estate	26
Who Can Say?	28
Allow	30
Seek	31
Truth	32
Shinrin-Yoku Haiku	33
The Trees of Notre Dame Paris	34
Coat	36
Rosa	37
Chaney	38
Kintsugi Bowl	39
Stone as Bread	40
Air of Abuse	41
Simple Not	42
Palimpsest	44
The Effort of A Word	45
Semantic Nuances	46
Olive	47
Maritime	48

Ampersand	56
Great	57
Lisbon	58
Neighbourhood	59
Finding Eucharist	60
Kneeling At Easter	62
Last Word	64
Life in Venice	66
Eyes	68
A Ship At Odds	69
Ethel	70
Easter Covid-19	72
Fourteen	74
Bede's Sparrow	75
Of	76
Arnol Blackhouse	77
Word Play on the Outer Hebrides	78
Christmas Shed	80
Litany of Lament	82
Times New Roman	86
Love Song	88
Hand	89
Heaven	90
Thirst	91
Gift	92
Prayer in a Garden	93
Influence	94
Holding the Sparrow	95
For My Mother	96
Choice	98
Foot	100
Beyond Grief	102
Low Tide	103
Balm	104
Clonmacmoise	106
Bushfire	107
Remembrance	108
Grace Notes	110
God Fails to Show	112
Tuning In	114

Slow Prayer	115
Home: for Mercy Day	116
This Day	119
Blessing of Belonging	120
Secret Garden	122
Christmas	124
God in Our Skin	125
Any Christmas	126
Bedlam in Bethlehem	128
Somewhere in Syria	130
Lectio Divina	131
Shrine in Word	132
The Alzheimer Christ	134
African Carol	136
Common Denominator	137
Five Paradigms of Celtic Spirituality	138
Planxty Aran	141
A Field Towards the Sea	142
Inismore - The Aran Islands	143
Postcard Aran	144
Aubergine	145
The Hermit	146
Four Hundred	148
Donegal Trees	151
A Listowel Saturday	152
Mountain With Lake	154
Good Friday April 1st	156
Memo For Easter	157
Resurrection	158
Garden Song	159
Souvenir	160
Coolgrana	163
Song of Mary Magdalen	164
For My Niece at Seven Months	165
Magnificat	166
Songs of Bounty	168
City Winter	169
Spring	170
Triads	171
Sky Sequence	172

Jesus of the Broken Leg	173
Vagrant	174
Connemara Noise	175
Perspectives on Poverty 1	176
Perspectives on Poverty 2	178
Perspectives on Poverty 3	180
Blessing of Farewell	181
Door of Mercy 1	182
Door of Mercy 2	183
A Baggot Street Suite: Blessings of this House	184
On Waking at Baggot St	185
The Water Vessels	186
Catherine's Room- Window	187
Catherine's Room- Floorboards	188
Catherine's Room-Hearth	189
Catherine's Room-Chair	190
Catherine's Room- Crucifix	192
Catherine's Room- Bedjacket	193
Catherine's Room- Cup and Saucer	194
The Chapel	195
The Five Punt Note	196
The Callaghan Room	198
Deed of Agreement	200
Tomb	202
The Illuminations	203
Sculpture: The Circle of Mercy	204
Welcome	206
It Claims Us	207
Proof of Being Here	208
The Long Line	209
Venerable	210
Mercy Is…	212
Blessing for the Road	214
Day	215
Monosyllabic	216
Utter	217
Mercy Full	218
Meeting	219
Need and Knowing	220
Before Sleep	221

BEING THE BIRD

Prayer for a Mercy Day	222
Garden	224
Knowing	226
God's Favourite Hue	227
Litany of Mercy	228
Friends	231
Be	232

POEMS AND PRAYERS

INTRODUCTION

If it were possible, if I could provide here at the beginning of this book nothing more than a good measure of quietness, then I would have provided the most apt and elegant introduction to these poems by Mary Wickham — that I can imagine.

This particular quietness might well include (at a distance) some ordinary natural noises: the small talk of birds for instance, perhaps the sound of a spade digging in the garden of the house next door or the sweeping of a broom on an unknown path — and it would be a very old quietness too; one into which many people and many creatures had come and gone for many, many years.

And then, having miraculously provided it and set it in place here, I would simply invite you (the reader and beholder) to enter into this dear old quietness, this fresh moment, without saying

BEING THE BIRD

a word to you about the poetry to be found further inside for I know that the small noises — the birds, the spade and the path would, in their own sweet time, do that far more beautifully than I ever could.

And upon hearing the spade you could playfully wonder, as I do now, "what makes that small noise? Is it the spade or the soil? Or is it the one who holds the spade? Or is it all three of them: the trinity? And of course we would conclude that it was the three.

And the noise lifts away from the three, wildly and wonderfully different from the parts that made it — lifts away and flies to us as one of the tiny blessed noise poems by which life constantly announces and sanctifies itself and pays joyous homage to its precious moments as they are born and as they die.

③

So it would fly to us and touch us reassuringly yet we might scarcely know of that reassurance – of the way in which our faith had, just at that moment, been held and nourished. We might scarcely know that this small noise (of the three!) had been such a beautiful little poem in itself – the sound of this spade being dug into the earth.

And so, playfully and with happy reverence, I wonder, " does Mary Wickham make these poems? Did she make the poem in this book titled "A Field Towards the Sea"? Was it Mary? Was it the field? Or was it that which holds Mary? Clearly it was the three and this to me is an infinitely happy, simple and redeeming idea.

BEING THE BIRD

And it was Mary Wickham who made with such delighted hope and resolve "To My Neice of Seven Months" along with the sparrow, of course, and along with life's great rapturous impulse to carefully cradle its newborn and dying miracles, with their suffering and beauty and to passionately embrace them with all that we have and all that we are.

Something lifts away from all this and flies to find us and hold us and this is poetry.

Michael Leunig
8-4-95

First printed as the Introduction to *In The Water Was the Fire*.

kite at williamstown

Listen, he entreated briefly,
letting go one hand and beckoning,
guileless yet conspiratorial at ten years old.
Come and listen.
A stranger amongst strangers,
the cool change racing up the bay from the south west,
relief from days of scorch, air an oven.
Crowds splashing in the shallows,
the widow-garbed from
the rim of the Mediterranean,
and kids born to the desert,
with their polyglot generations
spread here on the basalt whales,
sharing the green verge and miraculous waters.
Listen, he said and grinned with delighted awe,
as he chose me and my dog as his new best friends,
drawing us to the angled line of his kite,
child from a kite-less country.
We readied our ears for the sound,
rewarded with the thrum of the gripped string,
firm in its grip on the multi-coloured avian body of the kite,
humming and humming and tensing,
making a taut but telling music,
captive but free,
flung into the air and played by the wind,
a kite intent on peace and pleasure,
held and holding, rhapsodic.

covid-19 haiku

Pear ornamental
fruits only for winsome joy:
lofty guardian
*

long haired Magdalen,
the cherry weeps winter tears,
awaiting blossom
*

cheerful endurers,
red geraniums augment
the song my garden
*

pink budded points
flame to late winter jasmine
white warming the scene
*

laden the branches
ripe with the ellipsoid gold
of nippled lemons
*

pleasant but plain
jacaranda stands until it
purples, astounding

WONDER

It can, I suppose, be encouraged,
sought, yearned, but it's doubtful it can be learned.
There has to be readiness,
a disposition, but effort cannot deliver it.
It's more something that you walk into, are surrounded by,
encounter- an amaze, a grace,
gratuitous, fluky, a taken unawares in the best sense,
surprise the spark as
place, occasion and person accord,
an alignment of gift and reception.

I had read about the Pentecost petals,
tongues of fire rose-infused,
the weeping eye,
and another time I hurried in the rain to see the lace veil.
But at my first steps inside Rome's Pantheon
it was sound rather than sight that met me
under the vast inverted bowl made for godliness:
solo trumpet,
consummate breath mellowing the air,
each note praise of a tree- Handel's Largo-
the melody of amiable leaves
meeting the proportionate stone
and soaring, through the oculus,
to the purity of blue.

starling

Each afternoon, late,
a starling,
whose apparent black
shifts to rainbow iridescent sheen,
sings westward on top of the naked
weeping cherry outside my window,
incanting the fleeting euphoria of blossom.
Sometimes I notice, sometimes I don't.

jewel

Being inside St Chapelle
is akin to being within a jewel
or intrinsic to a rainbow,
but being inside St Chapelle
with the late sun slide-shimmering
down the vibrant glass
and a small chamber orchestra playing
even the most well aired of Mozart and Vivaldi
is, as my father, rarely effusive, declares,
"Magic."

Dance of the seagulls

for PMK

All the years I lived by the sea I'd not seen this.
Gulls of course, sometimes by the hundreds,
drawn by a crust flung from our gate.
Today a different sea, a different bay,
and you and I having a slow lunch,
not by trendy intent
but at the behest of frail attention,
drifting from plate and table to jubilant day,
gazing beyond the glass
to the blue, by the green,
with the Norfolk pines watching over.
Children and lovers, dogs and bikes,
svelte joggers and seniors out for an ice cream,
share the radiance.
What do I do next, you say,
you need to tell me what to do next.
I muster calm orders, one by one:
drink, eat, use the knife, spread some butter.
All of my life,
my mind has been able to grasp things with ease,
and now they slip from me like strangers.
Helpless, I am with you,
for whom now nothing seems what it is,
face value a currency devalued.
We sit in what is today's easeful
Alzheimic miasma.
Tomorrow your brain could hijack you elsewhere.
A little boy cavorts with the elusive ubiquity of gulls,
chasing and enticing, clapping them to flight.
Suddenly a shift to incredulity,
as he lifts a gull

from her slow-footed progress
and places his hands around her warmth.
I fear a roughness,
I see a rush in him of forensic curiosity,
but the boy is tender, as creature to creature,
and the bird tame in her dying.
The child holds her a while,
then, sensing she has lost her capacity for air,
he places her softly on the solid green,
she who might once have thought to die
with the familiar swell beneath her.
You and I watch the bird amidst the still jubilant day
as she performs her death dance,
the movement of her wings a last slow longing.
High above, the flock farewells her
in reverent and deliberate circling,
the midday sun casting flying shadows
onto the grass around her.
We walk out to her
and wait the while until she becomes
a
small
white
stillness
on the green, by the blue,
subject now to neither harm nor help.
Auden after Bruegel was half right:
sometimes someone does not turn away.
Yeats was half wrong:
hope does sometimes attend, hovering.
You slip your ninety-year-old hand into mine
and I shelter the bones.
As we shuffle back behind the glass
I wonder who will circle your farewell.
Will the sky cast comforting reminders of flight?
Will a kindness quietly cup your ebbing heart?

amen

for PMK

The name of the night nurse was, improbably, Fortune,
her eyes the only white of her;
the body in the bed was ninety and drifting.
This was Sunday morning, just,
and she would be gone by Monday,
a light-suffused day with blossom confettied at the window.
Now she was already a little offshore,
the jobs of the body jettisoned,
drugs for this, that and other guiding
the give and take of the remains.
Primed she was for the open ocean, surrendered to the tide.

Two o'clock and Fortune does the rounds, punctuating the dark;
pulse and vital signs, smiles at me, murmurs to the ancient one.
Three o'clock she comes by again,
having paced the vast building.
How many others are cleared for voyage this night?
She checks the respiratory rate, disbelieving, and checks again.
"I do not understand this," she says
in her crisp, acquired English.
"Her respiratory rate at two was ten per minute;
now it is sixteen.
This- does- not- make- sense." She gazes reverentially.
"Ah," I say, and laugh, none of us expecting recovery,
but tickled by minor miracles, so typical of her,
who all her life made healing.
I stroke her hand, storing the warmth.
"I know what's happened."

As much to keep myself awake I'd laced the silence
with word and music,

ending with Jessye Norman.
Nocturne, lullaby, lament, rhapsody, aubade,
each from one, one for all.
A one-word song, Amen, over and again,
a melody serene, earthed, becomes a bird ascending,
trusting the limpid air.
Amen, let it be. So it is.
I wish I could sing it for you:
it will get your heart beating better any time.

Three days after she died,
I dreamt she leant down to me,
Elijah-like spirit-smiling,
gracing her forehead against mine,
her hair luminous around her skull.
With Jessye Norman, that was enough.

gallarus 1*

There is a desiccation
that withers and deals wrinkled death;
the dim dryness of this place, though,
like the housing of tea or treasuring of flour
is haven, a crafted shelter
for the sustenance of silence.
Dry-stone holds the fingerprints of the ancients
who assiduously assembled stone on stone,
curve meeting concavity,
edge glancing edge,
each stone assessed and carefully struck like a bell,
tempered gently to the required space.
Not that it eschews water, being a boat,
but like the upturned dry-docked boat that it is
it uses water to advantage:
the distant but discernible harbour framed
by the narrow aperture of ingress and egress,
the slanted rain flowing off and away, not in,
water stouped to sign
on the forehead of the pilgrim foreigners
the telling cross,
a reminder that the essence of boat
is response to the endless ebb and plenty of the sea,
and that after the silence the song glints as it moves
from the half-light of Gallarus into the damp sun.

gallarus 2

We take the air, we say:
think bracing and salutary,
but also, by inference, proprietorial.
Inside Gallarus, where centuries of breath
have been inhaled and exhaled,
drawn in, held, and surrendered,
the air instead takes us,
encompassing,
infiltrating gently but assuredly
the meretricious carapace of
noisy industry and distraction.
For a time
the silence,
thick as the history and spirit of the place,
absorbs us
and we find ourselves dissolved with utter ease
into a greater air.
We are found.

Gallarus Oratory on the Dingle Peninsula, County Kerry, Ireland is thought to date from the 11th century and may have been a small chapel for pilgrims. Using corbel vaulting, it resembles an upturned boat and was made mostly without mortar from local red sandstone.

islands

The Uists were mercurial Dali art,
all melting landscapes and buildings malleable.
Water screening from sky to sea, a land barely there,
water soaking into bog sponge,
sheep hunkered expertly low to cope.
CalMac had muttered cancellations
but we made it across from Barra,
all the car alarms wailing
and the swell smacking the lower decks,
weird plaints of distress relieved only
by the island earth of Eriskay.
A youth on the top deck wore a parka
branded *The Storm Will Pass*,
which in the circumstance was a brazen claim, or maybe he,
like the sheep, was a native with knowing of the rhythms,
trusting that time would restore love-lilting.

It seems, when I visit wee islands, it is in the wake of sorrow.
It seems they will be islands of rock, peat and rain.
And sheep.
This time, already planned,
came soon after her death, not planned,
but inevitable at ninety.

You have to make a commitment to achieve an island,
the getting there half of it, footfall at once loss and safety.
The rest: finding the gold lichen that signifies pure air,
being companioned by little birds,

being beyond reach of the ordinary,
contained in an other ordinary,
by an other ordinary sustained,
and once, from a lofty cliff-cutting on Lewis,
gazed at by a lone deer.

Balm in the moment
is balm in the memory
is balm in the moment.
The extremis of small islands leads to extremis,
its dual cul de sac death or meaning, but not both at once,
and only one a coming back from.

An island is an occasion of pure element,
perception of the bare things that make the tick:
reclaim or die, salve or excoriate,
hope or hang onto regret and the grief that seeps.
Islands make you make choices.
All augmented,
the gleam of pink gneiss seamed with quartz,
some of the oldest rock on earth, it meets your palm;
the hard-won curve of scrappy sycamores,
deferential to salt-fraught winds.
These matter on an island, are message laden.
Reading is the work of the pilgrim.
Rock, peat, rain and sheep. And sky.
In the beginning was the wood.
Let there be rock.
Who made the sky, but I?
The eyes have it, what you see is what you see
and what you see will save you.
If you let it.

callanish perspective*

I met a man who belonged and asked him had he ever left.
I studied in London for a time, but it was so boring,
the city, that after a while I had to come home.
Intrigued by one who disavowed Johnson's adage,
I pressed explanation from him.
It was too dirty, too noisy, too busy and drear.
Mind you, it was Johnson, (the S not the B),
who derided the Scots for their oats,
now superfood, so perhaps his judgement is impugned.
Curious about one who was tuned to a different frequency,
I asked did he live far from here.
No, just down the hill, the other side of the stones,
my family has a croft there. We used to play on the
stones as bairns.
Ah, The Stones.
There's one that looks like a horse and we had a great
time riding it,
There's a veiled woman, a warrior, a bird.
Older than Stonehenge.
I met a man who belonged,
like The Stones to the landscape betrothed.
So, I came back.
I sit at my window, any time, any season,
and I watch the clouds and the light.
It is a different artwork every moment,
framed by the window. It is never drear.
His was a simple and brave trajectory:
went away to see the world,

found it wanting and returned to this remoter world,
though not to itself at all remote,
where another language is the currency,
another meaning what matters,
another way what carries,
and silence is the ground,
the gourd from which words pour and home:
a landscape scribed and tuned,
the keening and laud song of the ancients
cast across the valleys,
and he, surveyor of the Stones
and wonder unceasing from his window.

The Callanish Stones is an arrangement of standing stones in a cruciform pattern with a central stone circle. Dating from the late Neolithic Era, they are 5000 years old. They consist of Lewisian Gneiss and are found on the west coast of the Isle of Lewis, one of the Outer Hebridean islands off the west coast of Scotland.

bird in the hand*

Being the bird, I give a different take
from that the scribes make of the saint
stock still, unmoving and unmoved.

Raptor roughed I plunged,
until a tiny, sparse, tracked terrain stalled terror.
There was hurt.
There was fatigue from clinging to air.
Fear flared as I felt his blood beneath the tracks,
the life routes of a human hand.
I stayed.

To receive he gave,
his spirit making space;
to accommodate he hollowed,
the hand haven;
to upbuild he leant,
bending for berries and worms of the earth;
he touched feather-lightly,
for bruises incremental cure;
from his throat rose a trill to rouse the injured joy,
and he would give the odd tilt to take my eyes to the sky.
I became his prayer.

When the trinity clutch tickled his palm,
chipping their way to light, he smiled,
and once they grew,
and between my hale bones

the air vowed to lift me again to the greater air,
I left him, both of us released.
Each late of day in the valley of the two lakes
as the sun glances the heads of the trees,
I sing to him,
and he knows.

*The ancient Irish legend of St Kevin and the Blackbird relates how a blackbird landed on the saint's outstretched hand while he was praying, and that the saint remained completely still until the bird's chicks had hatched. The name Glendalough means valley of the two lakes.

word on a wall

One word on a wall,
what a word and what a wall.
Venice on a solid blue day
with sparse brushed white for contrast.
Somewhere along the Strada Nova,
as if to provoke the novel from any residual gloom,
some time postprandial as the world
and its generations walk by,
exhilarated by the day's crisp warmth,
and the city, albeit faded and frayed,
but still thrilling and still a miracle,
La Serenissima.
And there on a wall an artful act of vandalism:
was it a perfume, a movie,
an existential manifesto, a winsome name,
or what I made it that day
an exclamation of rightness, a potency,
of the frisson of being alive and wandering,
thinking of home yet acutely attuned to the here,
the past tugging tiresomely at my sleeve
as the future elusively strolled into the next *calle*,
beckoning with caprice and fire the next *embarcadero*,
just beyond the balancing of all the forces
and events of life,
more than the sum of the parts.
~ *Joy* ~
That night I dreamt I was Venice,
and its waterways my arteries.

only the best

for the mothers

        Only the best
        for him,
        the homemade fruit cake kept on a high shelf
        safe from the mouths and hands of teeming children,
        the delicate china, a wedding gift that otherwise
        became history in the glass cabinet.

        When one of her daughters, just fifteen,
        was killed in an accident,
        he visited solicitously, urbanely doling a higher care,
        divine endorsement of her sorrow.

        A bleak decade later a son was lost,
        found hanging from a beam,
        but it was another decade or three before
        she, who lived anciently longer than all of them,
        still restively fingering the beads for meaning,
        finally saw from her harrowed milky eyes
        what the priest had taken
        in addition to her cake and tea.

The Etymology of Relief

for CKC

Fracture and fall, fall and fracture,
whatever the sequence
it's a callous call wakes me middle of the night,
gets me driving in the pitch on rural highway
to find you also smacked your skull
on unyielding vitreous shine white
to set a secret sea of blood
secreting into already grieved grey matter,
the hip a snip compared.

A week later you stop
after a night of bagpipe breathing,
your silence shock salubrious relief.
I am relieved for you, on behalf, in your obliviousness,
dementia erstwhiled because of toilet call fall.
I stand relieved of duty of time of care of interruption,
no more nonplussed along with you where minuses ruled,
knowing the excoriating ahead that your head
has now rescued you from
was going to be worse than worse woe and warp.

I am relieved your disease was cancelled,
that you relieved yourself accidentally from it,
the inexorable fracture not of hip but of life
that was becoming more kaleidoscopically alien
and riddle rife.

You had become a bas relief of losses and lorn,
the who you were, had been and how,
indistinct by ravenous erosion,
the faint outlines on soft stone
guarded by those who loved you,
reclamation made honourably now you are gone.
Light relief there was,
plucky but futile resistor to the grim
out of kilter you knew in your unknowing
you had become.
Almost of guilt and regret and sorrow
I have relieved myself,
since your present exceeds all those,
flown as you are out over the landscape home,
your self your own again somewhere,
friend, in the gloried clarity of day.

ROSSLARE FERRY

It was as far from
Sybil Fawlty as you could get:
I know, I know,
Oh, I know, said the voice over and over.
He didn't of course, not exactly,
difference making distance, distance staking difference.
From my distance though, just a few breaths away,
so close I could see the pores on the back of his neck,
I felt the visceral truth of his avowal
and the undertow of close-kept sorrow
as he held his failed, fretful child
whose chin rested on his shoulder,
her face face to face with mine.
She ageless, frailly tumescent,
a macrocephalic rag doll lolling into his wholeness.
Her dark curls lustrously were her only winning way.
She would not make him a grandfather.
We were stalled in the stairwell
of the Fishguard to Rosslare ferry,
summoned en masse to return to our vehicles,
but somehow out of sync,
with the doors to the hold still locked.
So jammed, our world reduced
to an unsought sweaty intimacy.
My sea view of Tuskar Rock
and the broad sweep of the old familial houses
as we approached the harbour
shrank to this

out of sync child, her father and mother- strangers-
before the doors released us and the vehicles dispersed us.
Did he and his wife think their life would become this?
Days of grit and slobber
grudging a truncated future?
One foot after another,
one fitful rest after the exacting exhaustions
of one day's care
and on and on and on to the vanishing point
of relieved, grieved and rightful loss.
I know, I know, he murmured,
and it was about as close as you could get to
the honour accorded to kinship
and the sway of adamantine tenderness.
The integral heft of his words knew
that from the grist of care would accrue
the silky pure flour of love,
sufficient to see them through
and nourish.
And endure. Beyond the care.
The child's eyes- blue profundities- met mine,
and I reached out to touch her unthriving hand.

questing

The more the less,
the brighter the blinder,
(light from the source stuns the gazer
and obfuscates the shape)
the more reassured the less certainty,
the more conviction the fewer facts,
beware of tent building,
soak the fleeting Tabor light,
come down the mountain,
keep moving along,
keep sight of the Nazarene,
bigger than the mountain,
larger than a church,
the everywhere of everywhere
the Three nowhere caged entirely,
never defined clay-side.
Accept and relish
the quiet, albeit blurry, meetings,
breeze wispy on face,
peace at core,
a small smile radiating.

how

No matter how
low,
how lost,
how lamenting
it seems-
life-
there is always
the quiet
kind
beckoning
Voice
that says
-I share-
-I know-
-I am here-
-with-
-around-
-by-
abiding.

Real Estate

Before you view
Before you bid
Before you settle
Before you possess
Before you renovate
                   Know
this is the tree
this is the room
this is the other tree
this is the hallway
the bay-window
the backyard
the other room

that defiantly survived fifty years of salt air
and my father's pruning
to provide its lemony aniseed magnolia cups,
where my mother died in golden light
at 4.30 one morning of a March,
that enchanted us as children with its sheltering platform
and adult palate walnuts, the flesh encased
within a skin within the shell,
where my brother, three, fell
and found a scar more Blyton than Potter,
that was my mariner father's bridge in retirement
with its view down the bay of ships and squalls,
him avidly reading the weather,
where fifty years of pets are buried: four dogs,

and unquantifiable cats,
mostly strays who found their way
to a rudimentary kindness,
where my Irish grandfather lived for nine years of my life,
old and infirm and cared for
                                      Real   /   Estate

who can say?

The day they snaffled Gaddafi
from his sewer sanctum-
parading the parader,
berating the ranter-
that very day
across the other way of the world-
spin the globe and down a hemisphere-
a baby died
ten days after perilously early contractions
sent his unchilded parents into panic.
Held in the high-tech savvy
and maternal simulacrum
of the humidicrib,
he did for ten days stay,
but he was too soon,
and the filigree of his lungs
too flimsy for air,
so he slipped from them
to swim in the waters of elsewhere.

About Gaddafi's death there was debate-
its merit, its agents, the barbarous display
of the rotting body.
The way of the world a world away
for David there was but the stunned
tenderness of grandparents, aunts and uncles,
and the incredulity of the two who had made him,
caressing to memory the hint

of those barely cohered family features,
gazing at the flickering life
short known.

       In the volume of history Gaddafi wins:
       David's claim to archivable print
       but a few squares of lament.

       Achievement and meaning,
       power for good and for grief,
       duration and size,
       who can say,
       in the volume that matters,
       whose life takes the prize?
       A small candle's tongue in a vast darkness
       may tell more than the shriek of a million neon signs.

allow

Allow the light
is all
the call implores.
Allow the light
to flood
the heart,
to flow
the veins,
to fill
the space
that craves.
Allow the light
is all.
The light is all.
The light
Is

seek

"Seek the holy ground-
seek the holy ground
of need
where with the lonely,
the loony and the bruised
I wait.
I wait
with,
for,
compassion:
the hand, the ear, the voice
of compassion.
Seek and stand the holy ground."

TRUTH

for E&A

      Gaze at the sky;
      The sky gazes at you.
      Care for the trees;
      The trees care for you.
      Love the air
      The air loves you.
      Be still in this place,
      Let it speak to your heart,
      Speak to the trees and the air and sky.
      *

      You see, you are seen.
      You care, you are cared for.
      You love, you are loved.
      Trees and air and earth and you are one.
      *

      The trees say, "How are you?"
      The air says, "I care."
      The earth says, "I hold you."
      "Love," says the light.
      And you say...

shinrin-yoku haiku *

Stand bare under trees,
shed what has sore grimed your soul
and soak in green peace
*
leaf-luxuriate,
splash green exuberantly,
heal by tree once more
*
for warmth seek fire of
leaves falling at your feet
in undying love
*
stand under bare trees,
hold belief in revival
coax with love new green
*
dressed again, vivid,
trees lilting lovely in breeze
shimmy their richness

*The Japanese custom of Shinrin-Yoku, literally means forest bath. One immerses oneself in the forest environment in order to commune with the spirit and aesthetics of nature.

The Trees of Notre Dame Paris*

It's what the trees carried that matters
as much as anything,
the memory in the timbers of leaves and light of sun,
trauma and plenty, this flood, that drought,
aeons ago, yesterday,
all held in a concentricity still evident
despite being hewn at right angles,
rings of time seized with their felling but still readable;
and then their service to the centuries
of adoration and need,
lofty receptors to prayers and uprising of all sorts,
witness to the silence that harms, the silence that is balm,
unassuming hosts to the curious,
the dutiful, and the saintly,
timbers soaked with the grime of a city's venality,
infused with that city's aching aspirations,
a fostering intersect for the aesthetic and the sacred.

An unremarkable afternoon becomes lamentable history,
the arboreal code dispersed by flames
more intense than any candles it has known,
the solid nobility transmuted into ashy air,
an oblation on the altar of time and accident,
misfortune revisited all this time
after they were lost to the forest,
one element become another, released into the grief
and borne with the pernicious lead on breeze and river
through the city replete with blossom.

We weep for the assault and the loss,
we weep for the powdering of the trees,
when solidity was what we were accustomed to.
Would we have wept for that other wood,
carried by the One who gives meaning to it all?

We wait for this rebirth,
of the good ash being breathed in, inspiring,
of the good ash falling on other wood
through open windows,
the trace of a creative finger scribing in the dust,
sifting onto the moist paint of a late canvas,
one with another art,
or giving Rodin's Thinker pause
as it drifts silk-like onto his head,
the memory of the trees grafted to the people's memory,
waiting the moment when catastrophe begs for,
and begins, healing.

*The fire of 2019 destroyed the famous wooden spire and roof supports. The spire alone contained 500 tons of wood. The roof covering the main body of the building was known as 'The Forest' because of its long planks of 800 year- old-wood.

coat

for JMC

That the coat was probably threadbare
never threatened the tale,
and the fact the poverty of the coat,
combined with the earlier egregious and gassed misery
of the trenches of the war they called without irony, great,
whisked his impaired lungs off
permanently with the pneumonia
when she was only four years old,
only gilded the memory,
while deeply scoring ruts of loss.
He was and would always be to her
the man with the fairy coat,
the sunlight father within whose
coat folds she was enclosed
and at his prompting gazed through at the dust motes,
floating fairies in the dazzle.
Nothing was ever as dazzling again.

Rosa

for JMC

        The simplest gesture
makes for the child from harsh hardship
a diffident joy,
and makes the woman an acolyte of kindness,
who could so easily have consorted with bitterness.

The nuns filled their empty bellies of a morning
with bread and dripping
and the warmth of sweet milky cocoa,
the five of them marooned in loss,
their mother a too early widow,
depression in Depression.

She started school the year after he died,
and one of the brown clad nuns,
perceiving the lack,
gave her a doll of china face and hands,
the body malleable kid leather.
Already old, already loved,
cuddled and cradled anew,
slightly smaller than the viable human babies
she later midwifed into play.
She called it Rosa after the nun
and cherished it all her life,
antique emblem of care, a finite act of infinite echo,
a kindness she nursed all her long life.

chaney

I learnt a new word- chaney.
It's what you call fragments of pottery or crockery
lost at sea by wreck or storm
or tossed overboard in earlier centuries
to avoid payment of tax on cracked
or broken pieces before arrival in port.
Such fragments- the brittle, the broken,
the useless for first purpose-
are worked on by the receptive sea subtly over time even
as they feel drowned
amidst the weed and murk of the deep submarine,
as of them are created smoothed tokens of reinvention
delivered to shore after whatever time needs,
repurposed after the sea's work into jewellery of a sort
or decoration for a shelf with shells
or companion in a pocket
awaiting the caress of a thumb,
not quite a rosary or komboloi,
not a worry stone or amulet,
but a little shape of peace,
healed and healing.
I learnt a new way- chaney.

kintsugi bowl

The ferocity shudders waves of pain through her
and she becomes fragments,
riven by the blow.
She can still feel the who she was,
but each limb is separated
and a foot has splintered away altogether.
She waits in pieces
for the kind Hand
which comes at last
and lifts the shards with a measured tenderness,
shaping her as she used to be but cannot be quite again,
searching for the precision of curve and dip
to bring her back to being the bowl,
gently realizing the gaps where loss has taken toll,
where wound has quite vanished elements of her.
The hand works with liquid skill to pour the golden salve,
herself rent but cohering,
amazed as the golden warmth fills the voids
with the wondrous gleam of scar
which makes from her fault lines a radiant wholeness
and forever shows the miraculous visibility of cure.

*The Japanese art of Kintsugi is a method of repairing broken pottery by sealing the fault lines with lacquer and powdered gold that remains visible once it has hardened. As a philosophy it regards damage as part of the history of the object rather something to conceal or disguise.

stone as bread

Where stone has been bread
and many a chalice poison,
when Judas seemed host
and the tiniest guest mistreated,
how does Jesus reclaim the table
and serve not famine
but newly wondrous feast?

From the flour of distress
From the water of healing
How are we who sit bewildered
meant to make a new bread,
claim a new feast,
carve a trustworthy table?
The questions.
God help(s) us.

air of abuse

For all the Loud Fencers*

We all breathe the same air,
air is truly catholic,
and the air we breathe is toxic,
laden still with the fine white dust of death.
When your house is infiltrated with asbestos
you have a couple of choices:
abandon the house, demolish diligently and rebuild,
or die of the disease.
Well, the last is not a choice, it happens.

Asbestos is not something
you can get over, move on from, find "closure" for
or ultimately, ignore, because gnaw it will
into your lungs and the lining of your gut
and kill you.
And you, and you, who lived in the house oblivious
or ostrich- like recalcitrant to believe,
you are more gravely ill than the targeted
if you think to maintain the house as it was.
If you own the house, if you inhabit the house,
you have to own that you own it.
Once a house exudes the abuse of asbestos
its people can only be saved by
change.

*Loud Fence is a movement founded by Maureen Hatcher of Ballarat, Victoria, Australia, whereby, as an act of solidarity, masses of multi-coloured ribbons are attached to the fences and gates of buildings associated with systemic sexual abuse of children.

simple not

for PMK

She answers the phone.
I am too old to be in charge of this ship.
Too old and too tired.
Brain shuffle called for - which way to jump here.
Think, rewind.
Where are we tonight? Keep it simple, don't contradict.
(Ping. Oh. Light on the ocean. Take a leap.) What's the name of the ship?
Yandra.
(Of course it is. Right.)
I'm just too old and too tired to be in charge of the ship.
Well, you are ninety-one, my friend,
so you deserve to be off duty.
Isn't *Yandra* the name of the little steamer your Granny used to take between Adelaide and Streaky Bay when she came to visit?
Yes. She loved it, the voyage, the swish and the smell of the sea. And the skies.
Did you ever sail on the *Yandra* yourself
to get to boarding school?
Once or twice, I seem to remember,
but mostly I went by road, a long way,
a whole day in those days.
You love the sea too, don't you?
Yes. We loved going to Perlubie Beach. Once we found a whale that had been washed up.
(Tiny brown photos attest.)

Our Dad made a swing on the big gum tree at home - a few miles from the sea- and I loved to swing higher and higher to catch a glimpse of the blue in the distance.
I'm just too old and too tired to be in charge of the ship.
(Slippage. And again.)
Well, how about you go off duty now and I'll keep watch? You settle down to sleep. Are your feet warm?
Getting warm. You'll look after things, yes?
Yes, I'll stay on the bridge and keep watch. You have a good sleep.
Good night, now. Talk to you tomorrow -
we'll have a handover in the morning.
(The games we play with Alzheimer's.)

palimpsest

In the Land of the Locked Door
where Twilight is the Great Confounder
and Normal hides under the bed,
selected passport holders are granted
an honorary phrase,
mantra for un-mindfulness,
which becomes a chorus for disparate voices.
I'm frightened. I'm lonely. Where's Edie?
I want to go home. Jesus. I'm frightened.
Where's Edie? I'm lonely. I want to go home.
I'm frightened. Jesus. Where's Edie?
I want to go home. Jesus. I'm frightened. I'm lonely.
Repetition is replete with meaning,
meaning is more than the words,
words are the brushstrokes of story,
story is the colour of the life,
the life is the truth of the person:
this person is a palimpsest.
Handle with care,
Gaze with respect
the painting obscured but true.
Layers of life, layers of love.
Here is art that is fine.

The Effort of a Word

For Mae

    Purple she said,
    and purple she meant,
    and purple they were,
    the flowers.
    I knew a woman once, a refugee,
    who could neither hear
    nor speak the difference
    between the words paw paw, Pope Paul and purple.
    That's another story.
    This purple of the flowers, though,
    was a victory of will over assaulted matter,
    greyly alzheimic,
    almost every word mashed to incoherence.
    But purple, it leapt from her, it sang.
    She wrested it from herself, sound by sound,
    the first and the second lip-smacking P,
    the soft burr of the middle,
    and the tongue coaxing the L against the teeth,
    the vestigial desire to connect
    melding sound and sense.
    And the word soared in the air, resilient and regal.
    I heard it, I received it,
    as she had received the flowers I chose
    for her favourite colour, and we beamed together,
    sitting in the ancient, expansive ruins of her mind,
    at the endurance of purple.

semantic nuances

1.
A cousin visiting Melbourne from Ireland
found himself on a busy street waiting
for my mother who had ducked,
as was her wont, into a shop.
He read the curbside sign and being the dutiful sort,
He sat, squeezing with some difficulty,
and unclear as to the reason for their fractious glares,
between the two women already seated on the bus stop
bench.
No Standing it said, so he felt legally obliged to sit.

2.
Keep off the Grass it would be in the curt English,
a slow-fused but menacing imperative,
but by Lake Como it is rendered endearingly
Rispetta Il Verde.
Respect the green.
Apart from coincidental operatic echoes,
it evokes a concord of creature and the green,
a noble attitude whose respectful simile
is *onorare-* which seems to mean both to comply
and to honour.
Honour the grass. Should we not?

olive

What is claimed olive in cloth and pigment
is antithetical to the tree I see from my window,
whose leaves scintillate in silver flicker,
whose fruit has a dense moistness in its hue,
whose oil pours plenteous blessing,
the whole infused with the pervasive light and sea of islands various,
unreplicated in flat paint on a wall or the clothes of war.

maritime

for Mary Todd and Gerry O'Neill

The sea has always given to us:
to my father scavenging at Rosslare in the thirties,
down the cliff from the house,
even that named for the sea;
the driftwood and quotidian bits, and the hen's teeth:
a shipload of coal strewn in a never repeated donation
along the strand;
once dried, it saw them through winter;
a crate of rare oranges of tongue-tingling juice, conjuring
the sun –
this one's calamity that one's treasure.
What floats arrives somewhere.

Once a sodden pair of trousers devoid of corpus,
ten redeemable English pounds
in the anonymous pockets,
a fortune in its day that his mother
ruefully dried before the fire
and which paid for his passage to Liverpool
to start big life at sea.
Fretfully she wished he'd stayed with his early thought of
becoming Pope
rather than his held aim to be Captain,
long way from the callow cabin boy who was, though,
sea-sick only once.
She kept one of the crisp salt-scented notes
in an old tea caddy, never spent.

The day he left she gave him a caul to keep him safe,
her only child.
It kept him, by and large, and he kept it. All the life.
It is still here, inherited, strange little charmed remnant.
No idea whose womb made it
nor what happened to its veiled baby.

The sea has always given to us:
the Captain's return highly prized for the presents
for we three kids as much as his presence:
lacquered curios from Hong Kong and Singapore,
tales of Change Alley and Clifford pier and bum boats,
jaldi jaldi;
the New Zealand paua shell with its wondrous
purple and green iridescence;
the carapace of a huge Christmas Island crab,
for years on top of a kitchen cupboard
like a fierce red talisman,
until a cat, sensing residual seafood,
knocked it down into brittle pieces;
out of date deliquescent barley sugar from the lifeboats
that stuck to our teeth and tasted peculiar but gave the
sugar fix;
chopsticks and hazardous shark tooth sword
and lightning-tailored outfits.

And we, meanwhile, became beachcombers in our tamer
bay,
bringing home gracious salvage:
old buoys and lobster pots lobster-less,
lost from distant moorings,
driftwood art, sea-smoothed shells and glass gems,

and once an ancient one-legged seagull
who lived out his days
fed by our mother in the backyard.
Summers were swimming
in the natural pools with catfish
and the occasional sting-ray,
lissome slippery little fish in our element,
in sight of the house,
brave not foolhardy, and never beyond
the second circle of rocks,
with its pointed guardian at the mouth.

And still we harbour the treasures gathered before and
during our time:
the ornately carved shell-lamp from Genoa;
the whale's tooth; the Indian brass,
a sturdy binnacle, a ship's compass
rocking rightly in its cradle,
and the scale model Chinese junk of true heart teak,
made by a crewman whiling away the tedium time.

The primary maps in our house
were the cartography of the sea:
The tracks of equatorial currents and north Atlantic drift,
reefs and rips and wrecks and channels and lights,
the land blank except for navigation aids,
all for the service of the sea.

We were raised on the enunciation of lists of ships:
the Irish Tree ships, the Blue funnel Greek hero ships, the
Phosphate Tri ships-
Cedar, Alder, Spruce, Peleus, Jason, Achilles,

Triaster, Triadic, Triellis,
and the brave little Killurin the first,
way before our docking.
We knew as gospel that ships even of male names were feminine,
and nautical idiom gave us distinctive plosives:
ballast and bilge and bollards.
We lived not the nine to five rhythm but ship time –
at sea, docked, away, ashore.

My brother guards the life log-book.
Colombo, St John, Valparaiso, Bombay, Port Said, Nauru...
Succinct entries, factual and unemotive except the rare
signifier even in the moment that the moment was rare-
when he met our mother, a prescient choice of red ink,
loved at first meeting, and when each child was born.
Our mother ever reminded him wryly of the telegram
he sent from afar for his younger son's launching,
not his absence but the spare wording galled her after a long labour.
She gave him grudging but loving leeway,
conferring his name as the bubby's second.

And the sea, like its ebb tides, takes:
we would race in the VW beetle driven
by our enterprising mother
from the old Docklands to pause
at the river's narrow mouth,
the ship so closely gliding, the crew just beyond touch,
along Williamstown's island edges, and on to our house,
waiting for the ship to round into sight

on its way down the bay,
and we waved from the gate as he waved from the bridge
over and over in broad gestures,
binoculars picking out our daddy in charge of the ship,
receding to the horizon.
We never thought he would not return.
Like the tide he would splash back to our door,
bringing bounty.

No ebb tide when the sea took from my grandfather,
a young man of the Fort Rosslare,
whose houses it gorged on one storm
over a hundred years ago,
having nibbled menacingly for years,
residents scrambling in the January freeze
by boat and foot
to the slender safety of the peninsula,
only slightly less slender than the point they fled;
skeleton houses still sometimes wistfully
visible at lowest tide;
later, my grandmother, not without reason
terrified on the frosty nights
that the cliff beneath the house would crack and plummet
them to a wet grave,
erosion ultimately sending them a few more paces inland
to build again;
and their son, homes always by the sea,
addicted to the littoral,
mucking around by piers and harbours,
strolling the beaches and headlands,
hands patiently coaxing in waters various the cod,
the flathead and flounder, and the famous,

now hen's teeth, Rosslare herrings.
He saved fellow mariners from loss in storm,
all at risk in the fury;
he told of albatross and giant jelly fish out there
in the vastness where land-lack could unbalance a mind
unless one gripped the idea of shore,
of early on all hands nearly lost
in Penzance Bay in heavy fog,
of cargoes loaded and disgorged:
rice and tea and shoes and spice and paper and jute,
flour sacks with and without the flour,
timber, dangerous if it shifted, enough to flip a ship,
and later the phosphate that made of guano
agricultural boon;
when the hold was the only container aboard.

And he took his portion: imbibing
the science and poetry of the sea,
reading the stars and shooting the sun,
shore leave in places that amazed
his inquisitive and inventive mind,
same god different colour,
or sometimes too busy on board
to go down the gangplank
to put foot to novel ground;
once sailed, reading in between shifts on the bridge,
playing the mouth organ, studying for progressive titles
and learning to love Beethoven;
dispensing treatment per the
Ship Captain's Medical Guide,
and how he knew the precariousness of presence
as once the ship struck smack bang into a monster wave,

high as the sky, head-on, lifted and flung,
the whole vessel shuddered but survived,
all humans shaken and stirred.
At the last he was a casualty of the commerce of the sea,
having breathed in decades before
a miniscule shard of asbestos
that formed the lagging of the pipes
on the old merchant ships,
biding its time, patient, pernicious, to bite.

I knew he was ill when the sardines in Venice
had no taste for him.
Later days I signed a placatory legal paper
that if he choked, I'd take the blame.
A worthy risk as he savoured a sip of a rose-coloured wine
and a teaspoon of caviar, pure protein, little life orbs
bursting to the ocean.

We stood that last time on the Rosslare clifftop
just along from the ruined old house
watching Fergus in his clinker boat
luring gullible mackerel,
the sun winking on mild swell,
opportunistic gulls loitering,
the Stena ferry cranking up for the evening sail.
Home here, home there: a man of two hemispheres.
The pull of the old seascape had fetched him
for final embrace,
his people of the new one beckoned him back
to the reliance of the known,
to the love he had grown.

He had come home because none but his bones
knew he was dying;
We were going home with the tacit fact
that his life was leaching,
although I never knew if he knew he would not be back.
As the plane cradled us out over Dublin,
the pewter sea rippled expansive lines of farewell,
and was a great kindly shroud.

ampersand

(who became C U)
        The world turns this night
        as I drive home into the gloaming
        and the ancestors come out to play,
        the mother of pearl wash of the sky
        coaxing them to immediacy:
        their fondness and their loss,
        their shaping and their passing.

        The world turns this night
        as a little life works away in the hospitable dark
        and news of her holding is entrusted,
        she making and being made,
        heartbeat within cavernous heartbeat,
        a submariner meshing tissue and bone,
        endowed with this one's will, that one's nose,
        forging random and predictable kinlikeness
        and her vivifying, unreplicated self,
        already beloved beyond measure,
        the first of the next generation.
        See you.

Great

She made me great,
the girl.
We all overdosed on oxytocin,
for months and months
breathing extravagantly the odour of infancy,
such bounty after years
that had dwindled the generation that bore us,
the optimum of newness
strangely mingled with the previous,
a precious blend
of familiarity and uniqueness.
The first grand.
Her name has meaning in Irish and Italian,
her genes those with the Greek and the Scot-
what a polyglot and potent lot poured into
this novel human
amazement
who made me great-aunt.
I see you.

lisbon

The insouciance of the mind
threads and embroiders, joining disparate strands
that become tapestried in memory, inextricable.
In Lisbon when he heard the news, my brother,
then traipsing from church to triumphal
and crumbled church,
scaling anciently earthquaked ruins
and searching for dark coolness in August scorch
as tourist, became worshipper,
lighting votive candles for her as he went.
I like to think of the churches of Lisbon
illumined from within
by these small apostrophes of flame:
Santa Maria, Convento da Graco, Jeronimos, Estrele...
their dialect of faith different from hers
but in meaning congruent,
myriad candle tongues casting their glow
to sing her safe passage to the other world
as she left this one at ninety
across the entire other side of the world.
She'd never been to Lisbon, nor ever,
I expect, thought of it but fleetingly.
Her memory is now burned into its air and stone,
and if ever I get there it will be her, and my brother,
that will grace my view.

neighbourhood

The pelicans progress this
pellucid evening
down the coast,
their flight a synthesis
of lumbering unlikeliness
and effortless gliding grace.
They are on their way back
from a Covid-19 socially distanced fish meet,
finding the skies refreshingly free of the jumbo jets
that seem so closely at first glance to resemble them,
but in truth lack the finesse
and the nobility of the genuine bird.

Finding Eucharist

Some lament the morphing of Mass
that Covid has made, taking it from churches,
the cessation or forced dwindling
of assemblies and custom.
The elsewhere becomes the beckoning locus for Eucharist.
Holy Thursday and feet are being washed
at the palliative care hospice and the kindergarten
and the lonely little bedsits of the cities.
Holy Thursday, and food is being prepared, feasts created:
the friends meeting to make the year's passata,
carrying away the smell of tomatoes in their clothes,
the village in PNG using its donated cook-house
to enhance nutrition,
the local Sikhs in my suburb making hundreds of meals
for the needy,
the inner-city St V de P soup van serves
warm social contact for street-sleepers.
Jack is welcomed as the first family baby
for nearly forty years.
Breda is feted months after her restricted funeral
by a grand wake.
We laugh, incredulous, that someone on Facebook
remembers the name of a little dog
from Rosslare of the 1920s,
that starts a flurry of comments for families
connected by seafaring.

What if this Covid moment means Eucharist is not banned
but freed,
not restricted (or not merely so) but rediscovered?
Found in a different light? Seen in ampler places?
Every Thursday is Holy Thursday;
Holy Thursday is every day.
Holy is every Thursday; every day is holy,
when and where feet are being washed,
when and where food is being shared,
when and where memory meets story
and becomes love's utterance.
This is Eucharist, the Jesus feast, the Jesus table,
the Jesus company, the God memory, the good God story.
Is.

kneeling at easter*

There are no synonyms for the verb *to kneel*.
It stands unique, nothing else says it.
It can be an act of cruel coercion, gun to head,
but at its best is a gesture of wonder and waiting
and rightful creaturehood.

If you kneel at some Crosses you face the weary, holed feet
of the God we killed,
your kiss tentative recompense in the wake
of the Judas peck.
If you kneel before the great Cross of the Scriptures
at Clonmacnoise,
an eloquence of stone,
your eyes meet not death but
the first frissons of awakening
from what had seemed irretrievably finished,
as there your eyes find the corpse
beneath the substantial slab
on which the helmeted guards hold their spears,
all that heaviness pressing, pressing on the God we killed,
until the tiniest wren of stone slips subtly past and
instils its breath into the mouth of the cadaverous one,
who is about to rise, with the wren, like the sun,
for a new, transformed, but unmistakable day.

That's one version of resurrection
that meets the eye directly
as you kneel amidst the ruined green
by the great flowing river.

Bless and direct your eyes today
to what colours and what waters are yours,
and see what rising life meets them.

*The great Cross of the Scriptures of Clonmacnoise dates from the 10th century. It is part of the now ruined monastic settlement founded by St Ciaran in the 6th century by the River Shannon, Ireland. The Cross stands at four metres and is carved on all sides with sculptured panels, many recounting biblical stories. The resurrection scene is found on the west face, designed to meet the eye of the kneeling pilgrim as the first scene viewed.

last word

The words flew
one by one
from the cage of her mind.
A few fluttered, circling,
and some their toes strained
in fierce but futile curl
around the perch of meaning.

She stared at them from the windows
of her curtainless eyes
until the lure of air
fled them from her
and even stray fallen feathers were borne
on the air
away.

Two tactics calmed her mind
when it ascended into Babel clamour-
a baby doll, malleable as flesh
yet throwably sturdy;
and paper and pencil to make her mark
in a flat-lining script devoid of curves
and fleet of meaning.
Except for one word
rising like the trace of an irregular heartbeat
from the repeated plains-
a cipher from beyond cognition.
She, Mercy, wrote *love-*

Mercy her name, no pun,
for here there was no killing,
just the ambiguity of the wait.

Love- was it resolve or command,
prayer and yearning,
past or goal?
In the gnomic simplicity of her mind
it became the only word,
replete in the scarcity.

Nothing left to lose,
she slipped
into the restorative amplitude of the beyond.
They buried the doll with her,
hidden at the foot of her nun's coffin.
At the funeral the story was told of her scribing
and the word found flesh again.

life in venice

Mostly here it is water that carries all types of commerce,
and even the hearse, through the veins of the canals,
emblematic names for any life:
Rio della Misericordia and Canale della Grazia.

When you choose to walk the ground
of its one hundred and eighteen islands
and four hundred bridges
you learn most paths gradually-
Campo della Carità, Ponte della Liberté,
both life for the soul;
in quest for nurture for the body
you take the way to Mercato di Rialto purposefully,
stopping for a treat straight from the sea
at Campo della Pescheria
and on to the zestful colours of Calle del Fruttarol.

A whimsical and companionable diversion
leads to
generations of tabbies
and their balconied elderly keepers in Campo delle Gatte,
and for its wise radiance,
Calle della Scuola will draw you again and again.
Some routes, such as Campo della Guerra
and Ponte dei Pugni
you walk for a while till you learn an alternative.
Calle Eremite and Campo della Confraternita
bring solace in their right season.

As Strada Nova leads on inexorably to Corte Vecchia
at times you feel more at home
along the pure light of Fondamenta della Madonna,
at others the murkier Calle Maddalena beckons,
at all times trying to avoid the horrors of Calle Ospedale.

We all cross the Bridge of Sighs at some point no matter how charmed,
arriving by way of Calle della Croce.
Towards the end whether we want that way or not
we limp and stumble the Ponte di Incurabile,
then the hearse floats us out,
its route established and honoured:
always past the Fondamenta Fenice, which, multivalent,
as bird of myth and house of song, rises from the ashes
on the way to the final, infinitely flowering, refulgent
Calle del Paradiso.

eyes

For EJ

I cannot believe my eyes
we say glibly,
at once disavowing
and owning the reality before us.
But for you
unbelief is the credo:
your eyes are faulty,
flawed, perilously inaccurate, light resistant,
redundant gelatinous balls in sockets.
I imagine that you imagine
the splendour of green and shades of blue,
the versions of water and leaf life
leading the inner eye to vividly rich colour,
since unsight came late to you,
but still and all
the world without differential light
is devoid
even though you make light of the lack
and create your own augmented sense
of place and space.

You cope, you flourish, by being receptive
in an ably slanted way to the world,
at one with the essentials of the Little Prince,
trusting your other four enhancements,
and most of all, believing the eyes
of your sighted, celebrating heart.

a ship at odds

Incrementally
she moves down the slipway
into the murk,
sliding, with the occasional lurch,
not into crystal voyaging
but rust wreck and jetsam,
bilgewater toxic.
She moves from me, this old vessel,
less of the day, earth deprived,
more swallowed by inky sea than ship shaped,
aspects already drowned.
I dip my feet into the brine,
aching to accompany,
but they are waterproof
and the buoyancy of health
prevents.
She drifts from shore,
seized by demented rips,
a ship at odds with herself and her elements.

ethel

Left out in the rain too long
the words
on the pages
of the long book
of her life
turn soggy:
thirty years ago seeps into last week,
yesterday leaks into childhood.
When I tell her her husband
of sixty-seven years has died,
tears escape habitually stoical eyes.
"I need my father," she says,
he lost to her at eleven.
The ink of meaning slips.
Right feeling attends
but events coalesce,
all griefs one,
and mighty.

On a brisk, sun flooded day
we make a bid for the normal,
tricking the coded door.
Leaves like jewels hold and flutter
on the varied physique of trees
we pass on the streets
of the small town where
she finds and loses herself.
"Aren't they beautiful,"

she startles me with a remnant of spontaneity.
We share the ruby silence,
held in joy.

I tell her about her husband's funeral.
"The birds will miss him,"
her oblique response.
"Yes," I say,
holding in mind's eye
the tame and avid magpies
who came each day to his hand.

As the gold of the day pales
I lead her back
to the other side of the door
and kiss the top of her thwarted head.
Leaving her there, my mother's sister,
the cruellest, kindest thing.

Easter Covid-19

There is darkness. There is death.
Says Jesus, *I have known it.*
There is blockage and stoppage and collapse.
Says Jesus, *I understand.*
The predictable has fled
the normal has dissolved
Says Jesus, *I know. It happened to me too.*
There is fear and confusion and flux
Says Jesus, *I have been there.*

I am with you, I have been there
I am with you, I suffer it.
Do not be afraid.
Lament the losses,
Comfort my people
Honour the life
Cherish the loved ones.
Hope and heal
Hold to life
I am with you.
Says Jesus:
I am the still point in a spinning world
I am the life

There will be light, there is light,
there will be healing, there is healing
hope and hope and hope there is
There will be music; there is music.

*There will be life; there is life,
Easter is a love story.
Easter tells the whole story.
After Calvary I walked the road to Emmaus.
We will walk it together.
I am with you.
With you all.*

Fourteen

One question amongst others:
do shoes have **Two** buckles?
And why were the poor **Three** mice blind?
Four explorer's choices with infinite nuances
bring us, unless you are a stalled tetraphobic,
to my favourites, unblighted by age, the Famous **Five**.
Six is an inverted apostrophe waiting for a sentence.
Seven sins are not always deadly but certainly damaging,
curving into the piled zeroes that make **Eight**
unless care is taken.
Nine months to make a human unique in all the world,
present and correct we'll opt for **Ten** fingers and toes.
Eleven is a straight standing duo,
separate but contiguous.
Twelve months of a Covid year
seemed a lifetime but leak on yet into the next.
Poor **thirteen** so often atavistically excluded,
so often feared, hops us onto
Fourteen, an unassuming presence
fit for a plagal cadence or last line of a sonnet.

bede's sparrow

What if Bede had seen it in reverse?
If the warmth, the safety and the home
were not the banqueting hall at all,
companionable and redolent of food,
but the before and the after were the light,
with the in between more akin
to Sartre's hell is other people or Platonic shadows,
or at least less salubrious,
this gap we call life,
than the unknown previous
and the yet to be viewed postscript.
All of which sounds at first a bit grim,
but if true means we are intent on the light
and winging our way to Tabor dazzle.

OF

At the tables of betrayal
where stone has been bread
may Mercy prepare a new feast (of trust)

On the mountains of greed
where gain is god
may Mercy mint a new currency (of care)

In the camps of squalor
where despair scars the flesh
may Mercy lay a soothing balm (of hope)

In the houses of harm
where cruelty has control
may Mercy sweep its new broom (of justice)

arnol blackhouse *

Not what they looked like or sounded presents
but rather that they reeked, it seems, the ancestors,
of peat and salted fish and the dung
of the animals with whom they shared thatched shelter.
Stoop into darkness of stone,
mollified by unceasing fire, modest but radiant,
and the salvific kettle that hangs from the roof-beam,
the hearth the slightest indent centred in the stone flags,
everything revolving, devoid of chimney,
tiny light portal the midget door,
the whipping air rightly rationed.
Everyone, human and cud-chewing animal,
and the odd wandering hen this day,
is smoked, the eyes blurred to second sight
and the stark gloom spurred to story as it always was
by the tenacity of flame.
Stoop back out to the crisp blue and green,
emerge blinking from a cavernous world
to the limitless sky, the sea a stone's throw.
It takes me days to fade the smell
of the peat from my clothes.
Only the pure gold-lichened air of Lewis
knows how to deal with it,
attenuating but not quite expunging the pungency.
Part of me likes the idea of taking part of it back with me
across the world.

*The Arnol Blackhouse on the Island of Lewis is a preserved traditional 19th century thatched croft cottage built with a central hearth, no chimney, and no window. The human accommodation adjoins the animal byre.

Word Play On The Outer Hebrides

Where some would tersely say *Danger* or *Keep Out*
there is an expanse of phrase
one finds with the habitually laconic Scots
in the most unlikely situations.
Deaths Have Occurred At Reservoirs
sounds more like an Ian Rankin novel.
One is drawn first into an empathic fellowship
for those lost,
and then invited to assess the rashness
of disinhibited aqueous behaviour
on this tiny Isle of Barra.

*

The signs on Eriskay advise, unrestrained by punctuation:
Caution Otters Crossing,
as if they, like the pervasive sheep,
are currently progressing
east to west, west to east,
a busy traffic in the present tense.
I waited and watched, hoped and wanted,
but not one did I see playing quadruped pedestrian,
darting or scurrying
out on the rainswept roads and tidal causeways.
Next time, Tarka.

*

Some signs only make sense
when you have the back story.
Keep Off The Beach When Windsocks Are Flying
out of context is cryptically Pythonesque;

in situ you come to know
that this is Barra's tidal airport runway
where machines are ruled by nature's rhythm,
that the fine white sweep of the inlet sand
makes a firm compacted path and unforgettable sight,
in between diurnal drownings
and the quest of the cockle seekers.

*

In north North Uist, a sign on the guesthouse door
urges *Push With Gusto,*
and the wind and rain that day explained the need,
pusillanimity not viable here.
There was a hint in the air that
such an attitude was apposite whatever the weather
for the visitor enchanted by the landscape
even at its soggiest.
Push with gusto, be exhilarant,
live each small act with enthusiasm,
because you are alive to this place which is alive to you.

christmas shed

Baby Jesus, born in a shed,
said to his mother,
Is this my home, O mother mine?
Is this my belonging and my landscape?
He quite liked the donkey and the little lambs.
It felt warm and safe.
And his mother replied, Joseph's hand on her shoulder,
My precious child,
this is the place of your birth,
but no, not your home.
It is safe for the moment,
but moments change as tyrants change,
and we may be on the move again.
And Baby Jesus said,
So, where is home?
Where do I belong?
Where shall I settle?
And Mary replied, her hand on her heart,
You belong with the no-belongs,
your home with those who lack a home,
your friends the failed and the misfortuned.
Your head will rest on the pillow of exile,
your heart beat in each wounded heart.
Your heart will be their home.
You must speak to them of the lilies and the sparrows,
telling over and over Isaiah's word
that close to the heart of God are held the smallest lambs.
You will give them hope where no hope hovers,

*bleed for justice, gather the strays,
and one day you will ride this donkey into the great city.
Your landscape is the desert of suffering,
the mountain of need,
and the sorrow-tinged sky.
The vast sea that brings the fish
brings vastly too those who need harbours of peace.
You are not a settler, my son,
but a wanderer with the wanderers,
a kindler of love
for those who sit with pining eyes
around the campfires
of the world.*
And the Baby Jesus listened.

Litany of Lament

A Response to the Australian Royal Commission into Institutional Responses to Child Sexual Abuse 2017*

(in memoriam Anthony Foster)

Reader: We sorrow, we sorrow,
we weep:
for all that is lost
for all that is hurt
for all that is shamed.

All: **We ask your help, God of goodness.**

We sorrow, we sorrow
we weep:
for the cruelty
the secrecy
the denial.

All: **We ask your help, God of goodness.**

We sorrow, we sorrow
we weep:
for what was known
for what was said
for what was done.

All: **We ask your help, God of goodness.**

We sorrow, we sorrow,
we weep:
for what was not known
for what was not said
for what was not done.

All: **We ask your help, God of goodness.**

We lament:
the power that exploited
the power that evaded
the power that excused.

All: **Hear our cries, gracious God.**

We lament:
the innocence robbed
the fragility crushed
the vulnerability harmed.

All: **Hear our cries, gracious God.**

We lament:
the refusal to believe
the lack of understanding
the crippling of compassion.

All: **Hear our cries, gracious God.**

We lament:
the unwitting colluders
the incredulous bystanders
the victims by association

All: **Hear our cries, gracious God.**

If and where law was blunt force instead
of healing process
If and where protection of the system
denied care of the individual
If and where the inadequate heart
hardened against known need

All: **Forgive us, God of Mercy.**

Where we turned the blind eye
where we covered our ears from the cries
where we put stones in our shoes
to prevent leaps to defence

All: **Forgive us, God of Mercy.**

Where courage has been compromised
where kindness has been tepid
where mercy has been muted

All: **Forgive us, God of Mercy.**

From our lament,
from the deep keening of our loss
and the sorrow that is seeping around us,

we yearn to make a new hope,
from the heart of Mercy,
from the depth of the Spirit:
the hope of a wounded people,
the hope of hurt needing to heal,
a brokenness called to wholeness,
a ruin needing to be rebuilt.

All: **May God gather us in hope,
heal the brokenness,
and guide the rebuilding.
Only in God is our hope,
only in God is our healing,
only in God is the rebuilding.
Amen we say,
Amen.**

Times New Roman

~for the Pilgrim Survivors, Hotel Quirinale 2016~

Jesus wore a garment of blue wool
against the sharp Roman air.
I am a broken man
said he to the one in the red hat,
I am a broken man.
The Magdalen stood by his side,
her long hair fostered carefully
to wipe any and all tears.
Jesus wore a blue garment
from the wool of his two lost lambs.

Jesus wore a simple tee shirt,
that haunts his adult face-
a little boy, an iron-on photo,
permeating the fabric's fibre
like an irreversible tattoo that stains
what was once blank skin.
At once proud and lamenting, he,
of the little boy still growing into his teeth,
a shy smile before it petered out
to a past excoriatingly present.

And the long pent thunderclouds burst over Rome's ruins
And the rain pelted down onto the obdurate cobbles.
Let it seep the rain, let it sink,
let it sweep to a cleansing flood.
Then in the righteous silence
let the little shoots of green spring and hold,

finding, between the lost stones
and crumbled edifices,
the good earth.

love song

I thought it died once,
the spark within,
that fuels the heart,
that pumps the blood,
that is the life of me.
I thought it died,
and I wept for it,
for its death meant death for me.
But the tears became a spring,
a deep and pure spring,
and in the water was the fire,
a thousand lights and flashes,
and in the pain was your desire,
relentlessly questing, delicate desire.
And the flame and the fluid,
the water and the fire,
were mingled yet distinct,
one transparent to the other.
The flame was not drowned
nor the water dissipated.
And this passion of presence
is, after all, beyond sullying,
or sense, or measurement,
and is the love I know
but am so slow to learn.

hand

The hollow of the hand of God
is webbed with the world's story-
the lace of pain, the lines of love-
scooped by ages of hospitable grace,
pulsing with the cosmic blood
of the truest heart.

Safe and snug,
loved and learning love,
is the child who rests there,
a being repossessed of innocent trust,
infinitely, infallibly, cradled.

That is not quite what the good book says-
it makes a keener claim,
the more bold since spoken by Isaiah's God-
the actual speech of the actual God-
not resting in the hollow of the hand
the child,
but carved,
incised as inseparable,
cut into the flesh and blood,
deep as bone,
one.

heaven

Heaven say some
is rest and peace.
Others conjure it as dance.
I think it will be
a place
where incredulity
is both stranger
and intimate,
each day
an eternity of surprise
and delight
at the truth
that God's
passion
surpasses
our doubt and fear and insecurity,
and
in the surpassing
does not obliterate them as unworthy
but accommodates and encompasses,
heals and transforms,
so that incredulity lives alongside certitude
in the circle of love
God
Is

Thirst

In my heart is a thirst

In my heart is a knowing
In my heart is a stirring
For the land of my spirit
For the home of my being
For the voice of my soul.

Deep-drinking I will quench that thirst,
I will trust that knowing,
Surrender to that stirring.
Pour out your grace O generous God,
Guide me on the wise paths,
Embrace me in the grand flame of your love.

gift

'Float in fire
molten gold free figure,
become one with the flame.
Leave thought; still the heart,
listen surrenderingly,
receive ceaselessly:
receive,
lulled by the loveliness.
Remain in,
remember;
remember
my love.'

Prayer in a Garden

Sink soul,
Into the silence
Of leaf-grained awe;
the sweep and fall of the melody of adoring.
Praise in abandonment
To the ceaseless ebb and flow
Of the mute figure on the wood.
The ache of inadequacy-
How to praise him?
Be still though, and become
The adorer,
Become one with the diaphanous bird,
Feel the pulse
of the thickening night air,
darkness swelling.
Do not hasten, do not speak.
Join the silent grandeur of creation,
Obeisant, exultant,
Thrilled by the touch.

influence

If you are a stone
thrown by the sure
Hand of Kindness
into a pool,
you may not know
the full extent
nor ever glimpse
your widest ripples
as they circle and spread
and finds themselves
lapping the feet
of one or two or three
unknown to you
on a far shore.
You may not know
the circles you make
and the water you grace
but make them you will
and grace you have been
by the hand of the One
who gave you to the water.

Holding the Sparrow

Despite collar bells,
she is regularly adept
at catching birds,
my soft-slippered, swift-limbed cat.
At least it seems a grace
that she sometimes presents her trophies
intact at the back door.
Once I retrieved a sparrow from her jaws still alive,
vainly hoping it would fly,
as indeed a full-grown blackbird
I had once unprised unscathed.
But this little thing, although apparently ungouged,
was too great in shock ever again to lift into sky.
I cupped her in my hands,
hoping to warm her for whatever journey,
but the life slipped from her
and she left me behind with her
delicate boneframe
and ordinary marvel of feathers.
I felt hugely god-like yet powerless,
provident, yet helpless to restore
or reassure that there was kindness at work in the world.
I cradled her until the warmth had gone.
When finally I put her aside,
a spot of blood from her beak
fell onto my palm,
and her memory into this poem.

For my Mother

(1924-1997)

Carry her, O God,
this fine soul-boat,
upon the vast ocean of Your love.

Carry her on waters calm and gracious
to the island of Eternity.

Carry her on currents of mercy,
waves of joy.

She is a sacred, spirited vessel.

We vouch, O God,
for her faithfulness,
her kindness,
her wisdom and wit,
her strength, her suffering,
her zest for life,
her goodness of heart.

She loved us.

Our pain is great at her going from us,
but hope we have in knowing
she is bound for the harbour of Your Presence.

Let Jesus be there to greet her,

Mary and Joseph and all the saints to embrace,
and her own kin to welcome her ashore.

May her voyage to You
be buoyed by the love that we have for her,
the loss we feel of her,
and the memories we cherish in kinship.

May we have by that kinship
some share in her spirit
and thus some share, O God, in Yours.
With all our love.

choice

The choices left to us were not about cure,
nor even for long about care;
and so we began to distil from each moment
that remained
the intenser liquor of love and memory,
while swallowing, force fed, the bitter pill
of grief that would linger longer than her, my mother.

Two things became clear on the precipitous slope of dying.
Two things not so much spoken about as known,
and so in their way chosen:
We would make those last weeks
(eight only from woe to go)
a time of love for her:
warm light and flowers and silken music;
and second, that according to her wish,
we would bring her home
to her own place, before she would leave it for good.

Life is sweet, she used to say,
and meant it;
and we wanted to make her leaving it sweet in its way,
for her sake and ours,
despite the horror of disease,
the shut-down of functions,
the failure of flesh.

She came home,
and confined to her bed was already
a little removed from us.
She had time with each one,
taking love, giving blessing.
It was as if she were gilded with light
from another element.

We stretched time to its elasticized limit,
reliving in the dying
all that was precious in past and in present.
The old house creaked with bodies camped out,
young and old, around her,
and towards the end
the rumble and swish of her breathing
set the rhythm for us all.

Kill or cure, survive or die,
one thing I now know because of my mother-
from her and for her-
love is a choice,
always the best choice,
and it knows not failure,
and it does not finish.

FOOT

Le pied de ma tante it was that undid me.
Restraint and necessity had shored up grief's demands
until the sight of a bare foot,
nonchalantly hanging, crossed over its mate,
its owner reading Saturday's paper.
It had the perfection of milk skin that foot,
but betrayed its age in the joint of the big toe,
which carried the distortions of long use
and the child's memory of ill-fitting,
previously used shoes.

I said, *I am going to see her.*
I want to see her once more in time,
before tomorrow's crowd.
It had been two days since she left home,
taken by the grey men.
I wanted, bizarrely, to make sure
she was okay in the flesh,
to see her safe.
Of her spirit there was no doubt.
So we all went, my father, my brothers and I.

I looked at her face;
I looked at her hand;
touched both in the peach-light
of a music synthetic yet soothing.
She looked not so much peaceful as noble,
resolute you might say,
dressed in her favourite suit.

Drawing back the white satin lining of the box
I looked at her shoeless feet.
She would have been pleased the grey men brought us
cups of tea.

Months later it was my aunt's like foot which brought my
mother back to me
and set flowing my ample tears.

beyond grief

Light chink above me,
small incursion of contrast;
strangely sensate I am once more
where no more once more has been.,
to know such apparentness of day.
Not from the toes' tips, extremities,
does the blood begin again
blushing torpor's cold,
but as a surge of brandied gold,
suffusion of potent geniality
warm world becomes
from the centre
slow, saving, sure.
Such is resurrection.

low tide

Limpet-like I cling,
unprisably demanding:
soul-mollusc suctioned to your strength,
my strength spent
as insistent muscle grips
safe shelter in your shadow.
No geniality,
no courtesy,
nor the love which is pleasantry.
This is the passion of need.
Life-questing in fear I cling,
and clinging know myself grasped.
You do not let me go.

balm

If there is a use for the word halcyon
This is it:
Six o'clock on a windless,
sun infused, short sleeves afternoon,
high up on the cliffs of Malinbeg,
the silver strand below,
figures on the beach,
one or two along the cliff,
each one keeping distance,
solitary yet communal.

Me, the sun, the green of cliff edge.
Balmy. Balm to the bruised and barmy.
Green, gold, soak in the day.
Goodness flows.

Sheep defy gravity in steady appetite,
cliff clinging.
Goodness flows.
Silver sheet sea, the sun, the green.
One rabbit, then another appears.
There is no hunter, no hunted.
Safe place where all may feed.
Sheep may safely graze.
The Lord is my shepherd.
Fresh and green are the pastures
To revive my drooping spirit.
My cup overfloweth.

Look down, look out
To the silver sea,
Air unctuous.

What is curative in its own moment
Will be so on recollection.
Nothing surer.

clonmacnoise

The thirteen feet high *Cross of the Scriptures*
at Clonmacnoise-
Sandstone massive block divided into
horizontal scenes of carved figures.
A thousand years of wind and weather.
Soldiers guard Jesus in the tomb.
To one side, a woman waits.
Corpse prostrate, hard-pressed.
A stone slab covers the length of the trussed body.
Stone soldiers stand on the slab, adding weight to weight.
Dead definitely, the body under stone.
All lost, all lament.
But wait.
A tiny stone bird slips by,
flies into the mouth of the corpse.
A unique, distinctive little feathered stone creature.
A tiny wren darts.
The soul returns. Life, joy, amazement.
A small bird finds its way past the death-dealers.
Stone will fly.
Death be not proud.
Spirit will have its way.

bushfire

The colour of ash is death
the colour of tree is black
the colour of loss is bleak
the colour of pain is much
the colour of change bewilders
the colour of landscape is loss
the colour of tree will green
the colour of grief is shared
the colour of memory is comfort
the colour of hope will hold
the colour of life has changed
the colour of living will be
again,
but different.

Remembrance

'I made the poppies,' he boasted cryptically.
"Oh," I said, lamely,
lacking an adequate response.
Ray was his name,
but he was never anyone's sunshine it seems,
having been left to the precarious care of the State
when a child.
Rumoured to have been troublesome
(he was a war baby to an unmarried teenager)
he was certainly one step behind,
with a stammer
that still beset him as an old man
and tripped up his keen wit
and hunger to connect.
The large buildings
swallowed him for forty or more years,
and the red tape bound him,
scoring deep into his skin.
His life was a round
of making tea for a hundred,
and listening at night to the whimpered rows
of that conglomerate century
of the ill, the impaired and the misdiagnosed.
In their company he observed
that deviance, be it inventive or unruly,
brought the threat and sometimes the effect
of the old-fashioned stock shock treatment,
a remedy he ever afterwards recommended,

not unkindly, when confronted
with the fractious behaviour of others.
For the rest of his life,
despite official compensation
and a spirit never quite out-snuffed,
he needed to be sheltered,
having been sheltered too long,
but he made of his life in the down-scaled open
a gentle and genuine adventure.
"I made the poppies", he said,
recalling the highlight of decades
of workshops packing and assembling
pegs and brown paper bags and the mostly mundane.
I saw first in mind's eye
fields of them free in the wind,
then a more intense red fed
with human flesh and human folly,
then collectors on street corners
selling flowers threaded and folded,
each one painstakingly petalled
in rooms far from fields.
When I see poppies now
my remembrance is mostly for Ray,
veteran of unchronicled battles,
casualty of war,
and true hero of the spirit.

Grace Notes

One of life's innocents,
the mind of a child in the frame of a woman,
doubly cruel since the frame is freakish, cube-like,
the head massive but stricken,
simplest things beyond her,
she the one dubbed simple.

The new music tutor tried a new trick,
coaxing the class to draw "dots" on the staves.
On the line, he advised, *above or below,*
Make some of them clear like a bubble,
Make some coloured like a balloon,
Put a string on some,
Let others float free in the air,
add a dot here and there to nudge alongside.

She did as she was told,
clumsy in the trying, unwitting to the wherefores,
but content in the company and safe in that place
where she was a person.
She and her companions performed the task
with degrees of skill and ineptness,
splotching and smudging
and making their defiantly imperfect marks.
It took time, and at the end of it
the tutor had only scruffy and scrappy pieces of paper.

It did not seem a success,
and attention spans threatened to depart,
until the tutor sat at the luminously black grand piano
and began to render into sound the shapes they had made.

One by one he played
the music that had escaped them.
They came at the last to hers.
It was the most winsome and whimsical,
delicate Debussy-like, unlikeliest sound of all,
and after it was played
there was awe in the silence
as they recognized the accidental gift
that was hers,
and her.

God Fails to Show

To our usual class of those
Life deems abnormal
came a guest group
of younger wheelchair impairments-
head-bangers, constant rockers,
twisted frames and contorted faces.

We were supposed to be making ceramics,
dealing in clay,
making from the earth something beautiful,
but overnight the pipes had burst
and flooded the concrete floor.

Between the sogginess
and the double racket of clamour and confusion,
routines disrupted,
volatility,
and the thin coating of powdered clay that we all took on,
it was at best, it must be confessed,
a challenging morning.

We put newspaper down to soak the spill,
and it soon became papier mache muck,
but not before one headline caught my eye.

It summed up the disappointment
of a Japanese religious cult
whose leader had the day before foretold

the end of the world
and whose devotees had been packed and ready to depart.
God Fails To Show

it said with both mock and sympathy.

As I raised my eyes
to the human flotsam and jetsam
around me in the clayey shallows
of the ceramics room,
it seemed a headline one might be tempted to endorse
in the face of so much
obvious distress and difference.

What parent would want to make one of these,
and having made how would one know what to think-
blight, gift, curse or sadness?

God Fails To Show

said the newsprint,
and I could see the lure of it.
But somewhere deeper in the sea of things
there was a voice that chanted into the pained mystery:
Jesus is these,
Jesus is here,
Jesus is one.

tuning in

Are you alive in your spirit?
I hear you.
Are you close to my heart?
There is a beating.
Have you been with Jesus at the cross?
It is a hard wood.
Do you know in your being the depth of my love?
You say so.
Well then, enough said.

slow prayer

Into the silence that stills
into the stillness that warms
into the warmth that lights
into the light that calms
into the calm that loves
into the love that is

lead my noisy needing spirit, O God.

Into the silence that stills…

home: a poem for mercy day

Where the heart is- home.
Where the mind strives- home.
Where the body thrives- home.
Home- the arena of belonging-
for safety, intimacy and nourishment,
a place to protect and preserve.

We want to be at home.
We want to make a home.
We want to enable others to be at home.

Home is the arena of belonging, of right alignments,
be it hut or house, shanty or caravan.
It is the local neighbourhood of familiarity,
it is the nation and region,
your culture and the character of your tribe, your clan.
It is Earth.
Home- the place, the space, the base, no place like it.
Sweet.
We all live here.
We are human.
We are creatures of sky and sea.
We are trees and landscapes,
grass seed and coral reef.
Cats and caterpillars, catfish and catmint.
We all live here.
Cats and caterpillars, catfish and catmint.

But there are those whose hearts are adrift,
whose belonging is fraught or shattered,
their minds denied,
their bodies deprived.
They are in our small situations, local and secret,
as well as on the vast public canvas
of the world's strife and discriminations,
those whose homes are not havens but horror,
whose habitations are inimical to life,
whose lives are exploited and commodified.

We pray for those not at home-
    the displaced and exiled,
    the destitute and disconnected,
    victims of war and domestic violence,
    casualties of greed and pollution,
    the innocent, the stricken.

We pray for those not at home within themselves-
    those with dementia, whose brains fail them,
    the mentally ill, whose minds disturb them,
    the depressed and struggling rural workers,
    the long-term itinerants of our vast cities,
    the workers enslaved by venal systems.

We pray for Earth, our home-
    for our abuse of its riches,
    for our squandering of its resources,
    for the malaise we have inflicted on its creatures,
    for our waste and our negligence.

We long to make things right,
to be authors of remediation,
stewards of goodness,
attendant to renewed awe, having respect for every atom.
We encourage each other in the many existing efforts,
we acknowledge the many ways Mercy is at home.
Now, this moment of all moments,
we are called to learn new ways, to risk new perspectives,
in order to recognise the cries and silences of the needy,
to name and respond to what has so far escaped us,
to know how best to foster and preserve,
to enable what needs homecoming,
whether human, creaturely,
or one of the myriad threads
of Earth's fragile, wondrous fabric.

God of the Universe,
Maker and Sustainer,
You are the true global presence of Mercy,
Your Mercy infuses every part of every/ thing.
Every part of every/ thing.
Guide and free us to act
with your righteous kindness
and piercing justice,
to bring all home,
to be at home,
to be makers of home.
Amen.

This Day

This day O God
On all my normal paths
I will seek your joy.
This day O God
In all the ordinary encounters
I will learn your love.
This day O God,
In the unassuming and the worn
I will hear of your mercy.
This day O God
Through the humdrum and the tiredness,
I will tell of your greatness.
You are in and around, close by and through.
All that I see and do, all that I am and have
Shares in your being and is vivid with your presence.
Open my eyes,
Open my ears,
Amaze my heart plainly and profoundly.

blessing of belonging

Creator God, bless and affirm our belonging.
Jesus our Shepherd-Friend,
purify and protect our belonging.
Spirit our Wisdom, guide and enlighten our belonging.

May our belonging be a healing balm.
May our belonging be a supportive hand.
May our belonging be an encouraging voice.

May we help one another to create
the ordinary and the great.
May we free one another to speak the shy truths
as well as the words that rise easily.
May we respond tenderly to our frail and needy,
our troubled and uncertain.
May we affirm the daily fidelity of each one,
and our fidelity to one another.

May we acknowledge with joy the unique gift
that is our belonging.
May our belonging empower us to reach beyond
to welcome and shelter others.
May our belonging free us to live radically within the
broader arenas of Church and World.
May we treasure the companions of the past who shaped
and shared our belonging,
as we move together into the future with hope.

In the name of that great exemplar of belonging,
the Trinity of Love.
Amen.

Secret Garden

'Walk with me,' said Spirit, holding aloft her lantern,
'I want to show you a secret.'
Enticed by her charm and her certainty,
I followed,
the lantern lighting the path before us
as the moon rose in a cloudy sky.
It was a steep and narrow path just wide enough for us,
rocky, and marked with the steps of many previous travellers.
We came to an olive grove,
a high placed garden
rich with the promise of oil.
Suddenly I was filled with fear
and stopped at the gate that led into the grove.
'There is menace in this air,' I cried.
'Take my hand,' said Spirit reassuringly.
Something in her bearing made me trust her still,
and I slipped my hand into hers,
her grasp surprisingly strong.
'What is this place?' I said.
'This,' she murmured, 'is the birthplace of compassion,
the home of empathy.'
'It looks to me like the start of the story of death,'
I replied,
as there I saw Jesus,
his heart breaking, his frame bent by the horror.
'Oh no, you are mistaken,' said Spirit gently.
She moved away from me for a moment,

leaving me with Jesus in the darkness,
and with her lantern she cast a wide arc,
touching the farthest reaches of the garden.
There amongst the gnarled and ancient branches
a thousand eyes gazed out at Jesus-
the dearest, tenderest eyes,
one with him in the darkness,
looking at him from the depth of a kinship
they had earned too early-
the eyes of the suffering children
of all the world.

christmas

From the rich nutriment of *Rahamim,*
womb of God,
from *Hesed,*
the inmost being of God,
from the secret radiance of mercy
in which the eternal Three
thrive and delight in their threeness,
at calm and supreme in their oneness,
is given to the unseeing world
the mystery of Jesus.
From the amazement of a woman's womb
the unspeakable Word is uttered.
Mercy made human
grows to see the cost and the wonder,
knows in his depths the depths of all terror,
is at home in the kindest deeds,
endures in his heart the paradox of being creature-
beloved and victim, servant and Lord.
Jesus, mercy,
in the wideness of the world,
in the hidden strictures of our own hearts,
Your face is found.
Your gaze will meet ours.
Lead us to look in the right places
this year of years,
O Emmanuel,
God with us.

God in our skin

Great God of the immensities,
Word of the limitless silences,
Surveyor of the infinite spaces,
Now
Re-dimensioned but undiminished
In the awesome cost of humanness.
Awe filled I watch you,
Baby,
Jesus:
First breath, first grasp,
First suck, first sound,
Learning to be human,
God in our skin.

any christmas

Not for the last time
he casts his lot
with small children-
the smallest, in fact-
this Jesus baby,
this child God.
Which means indeed
that no human experience
is lost on him
and no indignity unglimpsed.
And even if his own home was safely sound,
his parents model, if somewhat unusual-
his mother given to weird convictions,
his father perhaps not all he seemed,
and even if in spite of all
he kept a purity of delight
in life's other smallnesses
of feather and flower,
still there is the truth
that no violation of the smallest human
is unknown to him,
forced as he was to flee for his life newborn.
So all the sordid ugliness
and threat of the world
was carried in his soul,
buried in his memory,
and burst from him that day
when his last words

came full circle-
the cries of any child uttered
thirty three years late and forever-
Father, forgive, they know not what they do,
Why have you abandoned me,
I thirst.
Any child.

bedlam in bethlehem*

Probably at sea,
not in what seems now safe straw of a stable
will Jesus be born this year;
drifting unanchorable off the apt Christmas island,
His parents having fled a horror dust bowl
near the Pakistan border
Or yet another suicide bomber.

Bedlam *is* Bethlehem of course
In a world which seems divided between asylum *seekers*,
and asylum *suited* purveyors of war;
with those who cower, waiting for the lunacies to subside
and those who as asylum *keepers* send noxious letters
so far removed from the true word
as to be the unintelligibility of hate.

Into the bedlam of the heart of the world
Into the bedlam of our making and unmaking
Be born, we beg you, sweet Jesus
With word of good; word to guide;
Be born to us this time once more.
Can we guarantee safe haven? Seems unlikely.
Do we need your precious presence? Beyond doubt.
We welcome you from our stammering,
inarticulate hideouts
To bring some semblance of peace,
Some touch of order,
Some morsel of mercy.

*the word bedlam was originally a contraction for the Hospital of St.Mary in Bethlehem, the asylum for the insane founded in London in the 16th century. Ironically, the building is now used as the Imperial War Museum. The word asylum has a rich history and it is worth noting that the original building plans of the 1820s for Catherine McAuley's House of Mercy in Baggot St Dublin describe part of the building as an asylum (i.e., refuge) for women.

somewhere in syria

close by Tacloban,
whenever, wherever, humanity's hold
 is splintered and stormed,
cries as one ascend
why and why and where in this misery is mercy?
After all is pared back and even the certainties
of so many landscapes are strewn,
from the debris a small voice,
neither rescuer nor cause,
claims the irreducible
and only truth:
"I am Emmanuel, God with you...
you abused and ignored- with you;
ignoble and afraid- with you;
fraught of mind and frail of body- with you;
on any street, in any store,
in refugee camp and hospital- with you.
Part of, immersed in, companion to,
shoulder to shoulder sharing,
heart to heart hurting,
blood of your blood,
with you, in time and always,
because born,
Jesus- Emmanuel-
because born."

lectio divina

The Word is the worm
that aerates the soil of my soul,
making space and rightness for seed.

*

The Word is the water
that drips patiently onto the stone of my heart,
shaping unsuspected the hollow for a pool.

*

The Word is the fish
I wait for with scant bait,
hoping it will seize the hook
and come home a feast.

*

The Word is the wing
that lifts the featherless me
into miraculous blue.

Shrine in Word

The great Incarnation page of the Book of Kells. The Chi-ro page. Greek for *of Christ*. A great sweeping X, and the r, shaped like a p, tucked and curled in under. Word became flesh. Flesh holy. The divine entered nature. All nature in kinship with the divine.

When you look at reproductions of that page, it is easy to forget how small the original is, and how amazing the detail and intricacy of it. You need to look at it with a jeweller's eye-glass truly to see the richness and facets of life within its reddish gold. How many spirals, how many triskeles, how many circles? A majestic serenity. Yet a great and marvellous movement of being: contractions and impetus to the right of the page, each spiral spinning and impelling to the narrow neck of the right hand reaches of the great X : a birth, an ejection, a release, a full flowering, set loose off the page altogether. Yet not a generalised pattern: here is a pair of moths, there an otter, sleek and black, poised over an invisible water, curved between two elements, its hind legs on the bank, its head and front paws watergoing, in its mouth a long fish. An odd set of creatures around an invisible manger. Nature in praise of the God become creature. Moths at rest, twelve birds, serpents and human heads. And a cat with kittens, or with rats, in a curious game with the Communion bread. Word made flesh. This is my body.

And they say, those who have studied such things, that beyond the play and humour of the creatures is a serious cosmic symbolism. The lozenge shape of the moths is an early Christian symbol for Christ; the fish likewise. Icthus. Greek for fish. Jesus. Creation sings,
creation welcomes,
creation accommodates,
creation incorporates.
Jesus.
Word becomes flesh.

the alzheimer christ

What he has written
he has written, he says:
a name which signifies this self,
flickers behind the eyelids
and eludes its owner.
Leave the sign lest I forget.

I am become a ritual
of vacuous questions.
Within a fog dense and damply cruel
through to the bones is hid
the identity of things.
Familiarity is a stranger;
Alien the ordinary.
Woman behold your son.
Woman behold your
son mother father self.
Self knows no son.
Mother, what is a daughter?
Have I a wife, father?
Why have they abandoned me?
Iron of nail anguishes my hands.
Brain affirms this time the pain.
Into your hands.
But nail is for fingers.
Nail, nail, fingernail.
Pink polish ring cut quick moon file.
While I thirst I thirst;

cup will come too late.
I of the half-minute mind
will not know thirst then.
Tip the brown fluid sideways and back,
Rhythm and blue china, dance and thrill.
Spill, spoil, soil.
Thirsty tell me I am.

They do not know what they do
these faces and hands which
hurry and flurry,
strip, sear, sear, search;
voices which obliterate my past
more culpably than I,
forget I was not ever thus.
Lead kindly light.
Forgive I will. I will,
Lead kindly. Lead, light.

When fails the recognition,
when your name is beyond my sounding,
when my prayer is my obliviousness,
O God of the creative future,
from your paradise of perfect recall
and mind entire,
remember me

An African Carol

These eyes are eloquent but sealed
(as the fate of the skull which holds them)
alive but fast losing,
lips cling to the leather mothermilk purse
whose widow's mite is spent.

Tiny the magazine photo
Which unprised my eye,
Infant face of dessicated flesh,
Lids laced with the diaphanous beauty
Of flies' wings:
A precise and deadly filigree.

Tiny the span here between
Madonna and pieta,
innocence and experience.

O young decrepitude
O new-born ancient of days—
What child is this
Whom shepherds starve
And angels weep?
Lullay, lullay thou tiny child,
Lullay.

Common Denominator

We make it,
spend it waste it fill it
pass it save it kill it.
Such power we have.
Mirror the truth.
It, rather, makes us and wastes us
saves and scars, pummels and prunes us,
spends and kills us.
The elusive, inescapable, intrinsic,
ambivalent healer harmer,
ruler, ruiner of all.
Time.

Five Paradigms of Celtic Spirituality

1.

The day before I went to see the Book of Kells,
Cork and Meath had drawn, one-all,
in the All-Ireland football final.
In the long-room of the Trinity Library
the tourists were reverent as they filed past
the convoluted concordance of word and design,
largesse of ancient monks.
It was the uniformed attendants,
Dubliners to the marrow,
who conferred garrulously
about the intricacies of the game,
of referees and rivalry and the next play,
their voices tickling the solemnity.

2.

In Canterbury of all places
I knew the truth of being a Celt.
The great cathedral impressed,
its architecture and history looming,
a proud and invincible building for God.
Nearby in a tourist thoroughfare
an Irish busker played an Irish harp,
making his living
like a tiny audacious bird pecking the back of a horse.
In soft rain
the harper's fingers caressed his companion

and her song leapt pure and exultant
into the grateful air.
When I think of Canterbury I think of that harp.

3.

At Rosslare Strand is my father's house,
as so many in this land a shell,
this one abandoned reluctantly
when the sea's advance made the cliff unsafe,
just yards from the door.
Within the walls my father's father built,
and near the salt-blown fields
where goats and potatoes used to be.
I stood and knew the relentless, expansive, bountiful,
Demanding presence of the sea
which gives sometimes and sometimes not
the herrings, the mackerel and the dulse,
and always her bold, inimitable beauty for view.
The sea which fed them
ate their land
and sometimes in squall and terror
swallowed them whole, the fisherfolk and sailor

4.

My cousin Mary Kate,
in her small kitchen by the sea,
makes each morning the soda-bread
which she signs with the cross
to protect its cooking and its eating,
and since the evening Angelus radio broadcast

usually interrupts her dishing up the household's tea,
that great invocation of the incarnation
jostles for speech-space
with what in other houses would be the blasphemies
of a harried or frustrated cook,
but here are simply the reverse side of the one coin
which is currency with God.

5.

Ireland is an empty place,
sky and earth and sea in elemental meeting
largely unimpeded by human touch,
humankind here the watcher
at the trinity's mutual perpetual greeting.
It is an emptiness inhabited, a silence which sings,
a place where relationship pervades the landscape
and blesses every bird and beast,
is uttered by each fuchsia and gorse,
and its own tiny trifoliate green,
and we, after all, part of the family.

Planxty Aran*

Blue the sea, blue the sky, blue the islander's eye.
Grey of rock and rock and rock.
Black the stacked curraghs;
Birds on twilight wire;
Black the space between the stars.

White the gull feather:
White Kilmurvey strand;
There is white in the goat's unreciprocating gaze.

Everywhere the dash of robin;
Red in leeside flowerpots;
Red the mooring buoys of lobster pots
Empty on Kilronan pier.

Lichen is spread gold;
So the hair of my arm in cliff-top sun;
Night-golden Galway pulses.

Blue and grey and black.
White, red and golden.
Rock on rock on rock.
And again.

*Planxty, an animated Irish harp tune moving in triplets.

A Field Towards the Sea

Once, in a field towards the sea,
In a place where all fields are towards the sea,
Down from Mainister House on Inismore,
Four robins, one to each stone wall of the field,
Sang an ensemble piece.
Too far away to catch their colour,
By now I knew their sound.
Seated on a low, lapped grey stone
Skirted by an infinity of grey stones
In one field within a myriad similar fields
And dry-stone walls.

Visual sense so anaesthetised, I listen.
Nestled in the grey amphitheatre, I listen.
They say birds are oblivious
Of the pleasure they give us,
Their singing a territorial statement.
I do not believe it.
Addendum:
Myriad: literally 10,000,
From the Greek.
Frommer's Guide claims 7,000 fields.
Tim Robinson says 1,000 miles
Of dry-stone walls.
How many robins?

Inismore–The Aran Islands

Said God, seeing the rest was good,
"let's go for something incomparably odd:
an avant-garden,
clodless, sodless,
hayfever haven.

Water, rock, rock, wind.
Pinch of salt,
dash of sand,
and so that their children
may dream of green,
plants in a thousand miniature
but obdurately alive guises."

postcard aran

On the leeside of a white cottage
near Kilmurvey, I saw,
as I passed by on the way to ancient Dun Aengus,
on a one in a million glorious late summer day,
six variegated cats on a verandah.
They were white and ginger and black
variations on the one theme,
all one family,
sitting there sunning themselves and
delicately cleaning and preening one another:
smudges and splatters and trials and errors
of a couple of feline generations.
Above them on the windowsill was a pot of red geraniums,
hardy plant for an Aran winter.

aubergine

Someone described the winter sea
off Inismore
as aubergine.
Now it is merely an indeterminate lead.

It is a fulsome word, aubergine,
three syllables requiring
three distinct movements,
the solidity of the 'B'
attenuated by the dipthong
and soft 'G' which loll around the mouth,
roll and settle.
It is a word which takes its time,
luxuriating in itself.

Sea as aubergine gives beauty
to a purple malevolence,
but does not tell the black purple
of swollen corpses spewed up
onto black rocks.

In Australia, the aubergine is called egg-plant.
Winter sea as egg-plant has not the same allure
and is too mundane for menace.

The Hermit

Here, at the top of a ridge to which the road clings,
is the edge of the edge of the world.

The light meets the darkness in this very place.
The sun, splitting from the black of the valley
glints then ceases along the row of roadside posts.

Sheet of light meets sheet of darkness.

I had set out in search of the hermit
who lives in hills not far from the road I have told-
a person becoming a prayer-
halfway on the map, as the crow might fly,
between the holy mountain, Croagh Patrick,
and the peak they call Devilsmother.

The words of the silent one had summoned me.
I went to her small chapel by a stream and sat in the thick,
pure silence.

I did not see her but I know I was seen,
the silence having stirred, alert to intrusions, then settled,
absorbing a quester.

I came away at last, lingeringly,
farewelled by a goose, a goat,
and that straight-flying crow atop a hawthorn bush.
The silence had given, but I had hoped to see the face

of the one who spent her days in that undiluted air.
I left her a poem; I left her my name.

Three days later in mid-summer Leenaune
where all roads of water and earth converge,
I met her, the hermit, amidst the crowd.
She looked at me with eyes that were mine.

Thank you for the poem, she said.
Even hermits need the occasional word.
She left me then, at the crossroads, on one of her rare
trips for supplies,
as I swam back into the silence she had given me.

Four Hundred *

Lough Doo was not meant for this
blue forgetful levity,
sun shining.
Lough Doo is best seen as I first saw it:
the vast, steep amphitheatre
a dichromatic study in black and silver,
drifting mist penetrating the joints,
water from a thousand water-etched runnels
flowing into the lough,
a hungry water;
the silver-sinuous road clinging to the mountainside
lest it slip
and relinquish the divide between
one element and another.

The only sound here is as it should be:
water and wind:
sighing, seeping.
Now and then bird or sheep noise
reminds you that you are not the only creature that lives.
Driving out of dailiness from Louisburgh
you are drawn into and down
a cavernous quiet mouth
of long water.
It is a place for solitude and silence this,
where only stone decodes the immanence.
Stone not bread tells of hunger
and cull:

A
cross of stone
roughly hewn
with words that ricochet off the hills.
They make no concession to a reader's ignorance:
you are meant to know
the power of this as the power
of a great myth.
These words
do not
inform,
they proclaim.
If you did not know,
had you perhaps not heard,
you will, after reading, still only know
that the place weeps,
that the lough water is deep with a resonant sorrow,
that it is
the deepest water in the world.
Being none the wiser you will be wiser.

And should you go from here as I did,
not knowing until later about the four hundred
for whom there was no oracle of foreboding or favour,
clemency a vain hope,
It will be enough in that time
to have read the hallowed stone
and to know
that pity has made this water
as black and eloquent as ink.

When you reach Leenaune

you will need as I did to sit alone
gazing the length of Killary Harbour
and sip hot black tea from a white cup,
and be glad to be breathing the steam as it rises from the
tea.
You will watch the rain weep
down the cross-paned window,
and as you sip,
wonder
what were their names,
the four hundred?

*In 1849, four hundred men, women and children died by Lough Doo, County Mayo. In search of help at the height of the Irish Famine, six hundred had walked the twenty miles or so from Louisburgh to Delphi where a meeting of local authorities was being held. They were turned away. Four hundred died on the way back. The name Lough Doo derives from the Irish dubh, meaning black.
This poem won the Max Harris Poetry Award in 1998.

Donegal Trees

I do not have the words for them-
these trees,
full grown they are, so trees,
solid yet spindly,
scrappy in the path of a wind
that carries the salt
from a passionate sea.
Six in a row, planted with purpose,
with flair and with daring
on this knuckle of land
on the hand of Glencolumbkille.
And they grew and held,
sturdy in their precariousness,
gracing the sparseness.
Was it compliance or survival
that habituated into curve:
six trees arching housewards,
leaf greeting stone?
I will ask the name of the trees
If ever I pass by that place again.

a listowel saturday*

He would have had something to say
about the Conor Pass that grey morning;
a last look at Dingle mere fancy in the sleet,
and the wind a caricature except for its bite.

The news was full of it, of course,
but it was still a shock
to drive into the town, grey too that day,
and be brought to a pause
right smack bang outside the church,
ten minutes to the requiem.

The last time I'd driven through Listowel,
some years before,
en route to a B&B near Kenmare,
the hardware shop had been spectacularly on fire
and traffic was stalled as the fire trucks wailed.
If that outcome was negotiable- and we were never to know-
there was no equivocating this timeslice:
you can't cancel a funeral, at least not indefinitely.
Apart from the latecomers scurrying black,
and the indifferent bell,
the rest of the town was ghostly.
As we drove towards Tarbert on the
John B. Keane Road
we were the only travellers at eleven o'clock
that Saturday morning,

and would be well gone across the great river
by the time they carried his body the same route.
The stage was set on that fine long road
for the third act of a drama
whose first act was tantalisingly proceeding without us.

In the ensuing days,
of all the words, his own included,
of all the tributes,
it was his wife, a photo,
leaning low and close over his coffin,
gazing through the glossy wood,
her two hands flat on his chest
in a moment of such tender silence,
that was the most eloquent and abiding
even in the farewelling.

*in memoriam John B. Keane, playwright, native of Listowel,
Co.Kerry, 1928-2002.

mountain with lake

Fingers of afternoon sun knead the green. What water has already sculpted the sun brings into relief. Grooved rivulets become golden tresses falling from the crown of Benbaun: a northern view of the Twelve Bens.

I turn off the main road, having come from Kylemore Abbey. Water's desire for water is evident in the deeply etched runnels pouring down into the lough, patches of bracken like rust stains defining the green. A rock. A sheep. A rock. Sheep. Sheep.

There is a white house opposite. Discrete yet humble at the mountain's foot. Kylemore Lough concedes the house's simple beauty, showing it its face. Also reminds it of its place, the mountain mirrored, looming. This side the reeds shimmer. From this angle it seems the house must be reached by water. Later I look up a map and realise that there is a narrow road. Pity, I like the idea of a house that has only a water-road.

In the lake middle is a man in a blue boat, fishing. Is he alone the man ? Ah, no. See the pull on the line, a submarine challenge. See the bird swoop the sky, curious. The man enjoys the sun on his back. Distinct but not apart. Bird, man; fish; sun; lake; sky. Sheep. Rock. And the mountain. Distinct but not alone. Communing. And me.

Man in the boat
your boat lend to me.
Read me the mountain
tell me the sky.
Let me be in your boat
my face to the sky
wind-shimmered, water-borne.
O man in the boat
It is water-blessing I need ,
water-promise I meet.

Good Friday - April First

O thou fool of all the world,
April duped this year of years;
Such an end to all your friends grand schemes
You disgracefully bring in your mute dying.
Seeming.
Such upside-down unexpectedness,
Such wonder out of wretchedness,
Such burgeoning from death's tree,
Can we sing now of thee,
O thou finest fool,
Friend.

memo for easter

Holy Thursday: wash the feet of an Iraqi mother;
Good Friday: bring a flower to the cross
for her dying child;
Holy Saturday, the day of waiting:
light a candle from the great primeval lifefire of Easter
immersed in the flowing waters of creation.
Light it for a humanity whose inventiveness
is so often destructive,
whose intentions are so often terrible
whose actions are so often horrifying.
Sunday, early, in a garden,
watch and listen for reminders of hope,
for seeds of faith, for signs of love...
for signs of love.
Monday: same as Sunday.

Resurrection

The first alleluias after the Friday
must have been subdued:
clear, true,
but with the ingenuous delicacy
of surprise and startled eyes,
gathering to an assurance
not yet quite rested.

This light bears the bruises of darkness,
tender at its heart,
not from any defect of birth
but intrinsic to its triumph,
forever aware not only of the paradoxes of the one
and the seized pain of the few,
who, losing him, found him,
but of the treacherous mediocrity
of the many.

This life uses the shards of death
to assert its green,
quickening from black earth
and deeply bedded fragments,
acknowledging with deference but no fear,
of necessity syncretic,
its opposite as ally.

Garden Song

In two gardens may you meet him,
But not one without the other, ever.
Although Thursday's moonlight
Edges the olive leaves,
The darkness augments
Here in this anguish place,
His figure bowed by the weight of the world
And the wood.
The second is Sunday's,
Where grief's refuge, numbness,
accompanies the dawn until the word is spoken-
Life's triumphant, simple token:
The name, the pledge, "Mary".

souvenir

My grandmother is a headstone with my name
in a Wexford churchyard three years before I am born;
my grandmother is a thumb-print of blue patterned china
that I dig from the ruins of a house
on the edge of a cliff field at Rosslare Strand;
my grandmother is a caul
from some favoured baby unknown,
still kept in my retired sea captain father's wallet,
given to her only child for his first voyage,
and got from a local fisherman when herrings
were still the haul;
my grandmother is a scrap of a tale told sixty years later,
across the country in a potter's workshop near Dunquin,
of matchmaking and intuition and tea-leaves
and the courtship of the potter's parents;
my grandmother is a photograph
of curly-haired winsomeness
with dainty feet, (unlike her name, not bequeathed)
sitting on a step patting a black dog;
she is a gold wedding band impossibly small
kept now next to her husband's pocket watch
in my desk drawer;
my grandmother is an unheard pure singer
and purveyor of tales,
of lively eye and vigorous tongue;
she is a wakeful fear on a frosty night
that the sea which had already taken the road
would take the house with a great crack

and severance of earth;
my grandmother is an undisclosed but tenacious illness
that claimed her.

I visit the house she married to until the sea's greed
forced them out;
I visit the house she died in, within sea sight
but out of its range;
I visit her childhood home, now too a ruin,
the farm driveway of rocks,
pink and green ovoids from the distant beach,
lined with an unruliness of confettied rowans,
in another season replete with its berry,
the scarlet talisman.

Startling a hare that doubly startles me,
both hearts race,
but not as fast as the hare
as it scarpers up the adjoining field.
There I find a fallen tree,
flesh-hued, hollowed, sculpted,
two branch stumps like the horns of a noble beast.
I run my hand along its silken rump,
hungry for a token that grew
from the earth and water and human provender of this
place,
in its body the age rings of my history.

The next evening I return and cut with a saw a warm
bracelet
from one of the arms of that lovely wood.
I carry it home across half the world.

The sum of these treasures is mighty,
but in the end the unsatisfactory disparateness of things
falls far short of what might have been between us
if we had shared time, even a little.
For now, for this time being,
I am endowed with a look of the eyes,
a hint of the tune,
a brush of the knowing,
and somehow inside me, vastly unknown to me,
her memory, unitive, flows.

coolgranna

Over the earth of Coolgranna's ten thousand acres
the sky was.
Its gifts formed her body,
its shapes intrigued her mind,
its hues enthused her spirit.
Her father named the stars with her;
her mother explained the moon.
As a child she wondered where the sky began -
how far off the ground -
and what happened at that precise place
where the vastness of the ocean
met its complement.
She dreamt that if her horse leapt
high and wide enough
they would be taken up Elijah-like
to taste the texture of cloud
and bring home a handful of sky.

Mostly the sky over Coolgranna
was cloudless and they rode within
the uncompromising pure blue
to which she gave her heart.

An old woman, and horseless,
she still gazed each day at the sky,
and increasingly wondered,
with avid peace,
how many days there would be
until she became one at last with it.

Song of Mary Magdalen

Man of dreams,
to whom my heart warms,
dares me to dream with him,
gently of hope he sings,
'Believe in my love,' he said.
Man of mercy,
from whom my heart learns:
his tender carings bless
poor, frail and powerless.
'Serve me in them,' he said.
Man of sorrow,
for whom my heart weeps:
life cruelly crucified:
grief-day, my good has died.
'Stay with me here,' he said.
Man of miracle,
in whom my heart joys:
the name is simply said,
he risen from the dead.
'Tell them of this,' he said.
Such is my beloved,
such is my friend:
Creator's son,
spirit's true one:
wonder of all the world,
Jesus-Lord, Emmanuel, Word.

For My Niece at Seven Months

I thought for you, the other day,
a desire not grand,
neither lucrative,
nor now much sought.
It rose winsomely in my mind unannounced
as I walked my way to study,
close by the university,
in a street sun-glinting and elm-kept,
air cheek-stingingly autumn crisp,
that I would wish for you
a due and deeply derived reverence
for the great simplicities
of leaf and bone and water,
as there I saw a sparrow,
full-bodied, earnest, well-tailored,
hop across the footpath
in reach of my feet.
He nonchalant yet watchful,
I paused and deferential.
For you, wakening one,
I wish similar fancies:
lifelong, untiring delight
in such minute acclamations.

Magnificat

A hum came from the earth
through my feet
right to my heart.
It found my throat
and used my voice
and my hands stretched
outwards, upwards,
to the sky.
This hum, so resonant,
brought all the under-forces
and led them, through me to the air.
I was the channel
between the earth and the sky and the song
poured effortlessly,
rich, sweet and rare.
It was not a reed-like song.
It was a sound
of the earth's vibrations,
a tone from the centre
yet one with the air to which it was uttered.
It brought with it all the hidden things:
water-spring, cave, mineral reef, seed-
all that is bright and bountiful but unseen.
And it sang this song in me,
to the vast lucent dome of sky,
to the moving clouds, all colours,
and the birds and grass
and the half-ring of trees.

The sun diffused
and slid slowly down,
and my feet rocked,
glad and grounded
as my arms begged to be given flight.

songs of bounty

Where did you get the idea
for a daffodil, God-
the splendid, deep golden
trumpet kind?
I would like the freedom of the bee
to walk inside one
surrounded by glory.

*

Blackbirds: how could one
put into words
that inimitable
staccato furtiveness of feet,
the astute attentiveness of head,
the touch of gold on the shiny beak?

*

Opening my balcony door,
I walk into the eyelevel moon,
a tumescent yolk banded by cloud.
Defying appearances it bubbles slowly upwards
and I watch, waiting for it to burst.

City Winter

Alongside the university
the black elms arch,
their upper and outer reaches
veined against pallid sky.

High above Parkville
a hundred feathered bodies
punctuate the grey.
The black-clad scholar,
his habitual downcast glance
lured skywards
by the dip and swerve of birds,
envies their precision
and their abandonment to air.

All this I watch,
and my own face white
in the darkening rain-stained
window of the tram.

spring

Black wood blurs to brown
as the elms begin to fur.
imperceptibly the softness swells
and the air quivers, anticipating green.

*

Light striking leaf,
Light-striking leaf.
Gold greets green,
the concord of creation.

TRIADS

Three fat raindrops
glisten and cling
to a bare outstretching twig.

*

Through the tracery
of a scarred walnut
three early stars
startle the dark.

*

Tossing crumbs with glee
three children
conjure a skyful of gulls.

*

Three cheers for the heart.
Three cheers for the Maker.
Sufficient for the day is the wonder therein.

sky sequence

Wedgewood blue solidity,
immanence of sun;
banks of Rubens voluptuousness
billowing opulence.

*

Featherness, brush touch discernible;
whispy capricious frolic
teasing the impassive blue.

*

Imminent fulmination;
ominous birdquiet darkening,
platoons poised.

*

navy turgidity, sky rust,
partner to the city's effluence,
a weird rottenness rolling.

*

Quite inside the white,
window wonder seat;
waves of penetrable volatility
elusively gathered.

Jesus of the Broken Leg*

(Corpus Christi Greenvale)
He is the more than crucified,
The worse than dead.
He knows the day's hunger;
He feels the night's anger.
He lives the city's misery;
He bears the streets' treachery.
We do not meet him in the churches;
We would not want him in our houses.
He does not smell pleasant;
He does not speak politeness.
You will spot him under bridges;
You will find him in the gutter.
Greet him.
He is our shame and our reminder.

---

* Corpus Christi is a community of homeless alcoholic men. The crucifix in the chapel has been damaged, the plaster leg smashed, revealing the wire "bone" underneath. Above the crucifix are printed one of the seven last words of Christ, "I thirst."

Vagrant

I am the mad one you will not shelter;
I am the beggar you will not own;
I am the ranter, the intemperate raver;
I am the self you hurl from home.
My passion frightens and dismays you,
I am garrulously obscene and wild.
My rage your own unleashes for view;
I am your wilful, untameable child.
Reject, deny, revile, deride me-
until you embrace me I am bound;
my need will cry till I am free,
you are lost unless I am found.

connemara noise

It will seem like silence
when you first step into it:
porous, soaking up sound:
but becomes before long
an opportune space
lending slightest sound triple value,
enveloping,
sending sound you normally cannot catch:
wind in the spider web in the heather,
and in the heather
the tinkling of
a thousand thousand
tiny pink bells.

PERSPECTIVES ON POVERTY - 1

Down by the tree of knowledge,
the park end of Gertrude Street,
Fred was there, aggressively derelict,
on his clothes the accretions
of a thousand meals, drinks, dust and spills.
- Are you well off? he prods.
- A sheepish, yes, I suppose so.
- Do you live in a big house?
- Yes.
- I suppose you have a car?
- Ditto.
- Nice furniture?
- Well...
- Maybe even a boat?
- And a garden?
Guilt, confusion, hasty reassessment
of what had become a shaky interaction.
Ah-ha, said Fred, drawing out the vowels with flourish,
you are not as well off as I am.
There is one thing you lack, he declaimed
with a sweeping gesture
as he turned to survey the scene behind.
You do not have, as I have,
this magnificent fountain
(a Victorian extravaganza)
cascading in your garden.
The boldness of his gesture
matched the truth of his words,

caught the curve and fall,
the grace and the light
of water on water and water.

Perspectives on Poverty - 2

In the middle of a Melbourne
Refuge for the homeless
carrot shavings curl grittily
onto a silver sink.
My fingers soak in the stain.
Peter's brain damage
has lent him
a free-flowing, unceasing,
impervious loquacity.
He has always been a word man:
worked as a sports journalist.
So many cask wines and brain cells later,
his life is a betting agent and pub crawl
with occasional gutter fall.
He talks; I listen.
He talks; I peel carrots.
From memory's medley of fact and enhancement
He talks courses and horses
and of a journey to Ireland
with trainers and jockeys.
You know, he says to me,
the most extraordinary thing about Ireland
Is the depth of the silence,
the remarkable silence.
Yes.
It is an aptitude of air
unique to the place
that permeates the blood, the bone,

each cell, each one, aerating the soul.
And in moments of simplicity
at sink with carrots,
its grace works, a world away, for both of us.

Perspectives on Poverty - 3

The government department said,
'These are the social security and pension numbers.'
>   *File them.*

The sociologist said,
'These are the marginalized, the economically challenged.'
>   *Label them.*

The charitable organization said,
'These are the needy, the underprivileged.'
>   *Give to them.*

The guru said,
'These are the vulnerable, the broken.'
>   *Help them.*

Jesus said,
'These are my friends.'
>   *Join us.*

blessing of farewell

The tender Mercy of God has given us one another.
You arrived a stranger; you leave as a friend.
Our spirits are connected;
you have blessed our being with your presence.
You carry our stories in your heart.
We now bless you for your journey.

May this oil of mercy be a healing balm.
May this oil of mercy be a soothing rest.
May this oil of mercy be a rousing to renewed life.
May this oil of mercy be gentle closure for this time
and free you for a fine future.

The God of the infinite spaces
is the intimate guest of your heart.
May you be blessed with the certainty
that nothing can damage that.
The compassionate miracle called Jesus
is your companion and teacher.
May you be blessed with the joy and reassurance
of his fidelity.
The unpredictable, elusive but pervasive Spirit
is your animator and guide.
May you trust the path that is opening now
before you and walk on
in the integrity of your being,
within the truth and love of the great Trinity.
Amen.

The Door of Mercy 1

The Door of Mercy is double-hinged,
swinging in, opening out, sturdy, yet easily moved.
My friend says: *You only have to knock once,*
and you only have to knock lightly.
The Door of Mercy rests on the threshold of need.
Its single key is kindness, which is always in the lock.
Faithfulness is its lintel,
hope and healing the strong jambs either side.
The Door of Mercy might be splendidly red,
it could be an unobtrusive brown.
It will need to be carefully handled and its fittings are locally sourced.
Mostly the Door of Mercy stands ajar.
In spirit and in flesh you cross its threshold each day,
often unmindful, but sometimes,
increasingly, amazed at its potent familiarity.
The smell of the food of home wafts out,
the blood of the wounds of the earth flows in.
It is not immediately apparent
which side is which of the Door of Mercy,
since they interchange fluidly,
pain and promise etched sharply on both.
Blessing is for all who come and go, stay and return,
helper and helped, all belonging, each bestowing.
My friend says: *You only have to knock once,*
and you only have to knock lightly.
The God of Mercy, whose door it is,
is always home.

The Door of Mercy 2 *

The great door in Rome has been sealed,
jubilee reverts to ordinary,
and the surge of Mercy words subside to calmer waters.
But we, who are claimed by the word and carry it as name,
we will stir the waters and make yet the ordinary jubilant,
since every year is of God's favour,
every day waits for mercy.
We will not close the Door of Mercy.
We will stand as keepers, attuned, disposed.
We will hold the door ajar
for the desperate and the disruptive,
the stray, the strange,
the wounded wise and the child too soon old.
They are looking for the door,
waiting by the door, hoping for the door,
and we must, with them, and for them, keep faith.
We will not close the Door of Mercy.
There will be room at our inn,
we will make space at the table,
the cooking pot holds ample.
Through the door is feast and safety,
hope and shelter.
My friend, one of the wounded wise, says:
*You only have to knock once
and you only have to knock lightly.
The God of mercy, whose door it is,
is always home.*

*The opening and closing of the door refer to the official Jubilee Year of Mercy, 2016, and the ritual of the Sancta Porta at St Peter's Basilica.

A Baggot Street Suite

POEMS FROM THE FIRST CONVENT OF MERCY,

The House built by Catherine McAuley in Dublin

May the blessings of this house-
A house
Imagined in unlikeliness,
Dreamt with daring,
Built with love,
Founded on mercy-

Speak to your spirit
In whatever room in the world you are reading,
In whatever place you are called to mercy.

on waking at baggot st

(To The Sound of the Rill*)
Open your eyes to the new day's light
open your heart to the grace that flows to you
in a stream of life, a stream from love's very source.
Mercy-water is a pure spring,
to wash, to bless, to drink,
a water that is life,
a water that heals and refreshes.
In the drought time the thirst time
the empty cup time,
the absolutely there is nothing left to give time
when the throat is dry and no rain shows
(not an Irish thought, this!)
remember the distant
gently coursing
universal water that
is
mercy.
Let your spirit drink.

In the desert of urban concrete
is heard a tiny watercourse,
in the wilderness of forsakengod age
a spring of godlife flows.

**A feature of the back garden of Mercy International Centre, the rill was significant at the opening in 1994 when representatives from all over the world carried water to it in specially made vessels, symbolising each nation in which Sisters of Mercy live and work.*

The Water Vessels

Vessels of clay,
one a real sea-shaped fluted shell;
one gourd-like, smoothly black;
one carries the smell of rain on heather and bogland;
one polished and refined in its glaze;
one a knobblywild passionate ocean-wrested elemental struggle
with spume and wave and storm;
comes then the scent of red desert and eucalypt,
and there the delicate scent of the many petalled rose,
and one for all the world an inverted bowl
like a magnanimous breast:

I am looking at these;
I am looking at Mercy;
I am looking at us,
the one and the many,
the each and the every,
clay vessels treasure laden,
the body of Christ.

Catherine's Room - Window

The warmth of a late summer Dublin evening
reaches across acres of Georgian chimneypots
and
flows
through two vast rectangles of
light
as I sit in the room
in which a woman died
one hundred and eighty years ago.
I am awed at the mystery of her calling,
the grace which grew in her.
What is she to me and I to her?
She is present but elusive: I know her and do not know
her.
She leaves broad brush strokes
not minute disclosures,
her person less discernible than her spirit and her purpose.
Not for our times, not for words, so much of
who this Catherine was, it seems.
I ask for some glimmer of knowing,
some small window on her spirit,
a blessing as I sit here,
of kinship and connection,
of mentor and sister-guide,
of bonds across time,
a mercy shared.

Catherine's Room - The Floorboards

In a floor pared back and laid bare
the texture of history is seen in
mellow wood
from some long distant tree.
The knotholes and indentations of countless feet,
the secret dust which fell despite best cleaning
into cracks
are
storymarks of mercy
in this special room in this special house.

Catherine's Room - at the Hearth

Kindle within us, O God,
the fire of your mercy.

Make mercy spark within each heart that comes here,
attune us to the spirit of gracious Catherine
each one of us the hearth of your love,
Make of us warmth from cold stone.
From the long-pressed earth-hewn hidden-life
of the peat of our being
Make mercy blaze.

In all our works,
in all our ways,
make it O God
a flame that gathers and welcomes,
comforts and encourages
drawing forth the songs of the soul,
the songs of the soul of the world,
lament and blessing,
praise and lullaby.

Catherine's Room - a Chair*

It is one of several in this room where she died
and has travelled a long way
from tree in India
where they say it was crafted to order,
(was it symbolically oak?)
across oceans to Coolock demesne
and a lifetime later to its new Dublin home.

Just an ordinary little chair, delicate now from age-
you are warned not to test it-
not unpleasing to the eye,
functional, unassuming.

Is there not sometimes about Mercy-
the very art of its expression
and flourishing-
a delicacy and precariousness as this chair
that will not bear a heavy frame,
that would not survive the full weight
of law or custom
or the brunt of economic rationalism?

Is not Mercy sometimes a little chair
whose authority lies in its very delicacy
and its small faithfulness
of being in a room such as this day after day
while the drama of one life or two
is played out around it?

Consider a chair:
place of rest, waiting-post,
point of authority,
creator of the wide and commodious lap
in which a child can trust.

Do you see the Mercy seat?
Can you balance your weight to find rest
so that the chair will not collapse,
and become at the same time
that wide and commodious lap?
Such is the challenge of mercy.

(This chair and its companion have more recently been moved to the Callaghan room)

Catherine's Room – Before the Crucifix

Kneel here and what do you look at
but the cross that she not only looked at
but truly saw;
upon which she gazed with unveiled eyes
and a mind which made of it
not a devotional icon merely
but the heart, the nub, the drive,
the sense:

of all the world's pained and deprived ingathered into
the solidarity of the suffering God;

of compassion transfigured beyond human exchange
into the mystery of the needy God;

of grief not denied but given hope beyond today,
of loss not escaped but released
beyond its own definitions
by the life of the God-man who died on the Friday
and was alive on the Sunday.

Teach me Catherine the truth of the cross,
guide me always to stand by it in faith.

* the large wooden crucifix before which you kneel is thought to have been a gift to Catherine from her good friend Fr. Armstrong, and came originally from France.

Catherine's Room - The Bedjacket

I am caught by surprise at how small this garment,
how worn and fragile.
It brings me close to the woman who wore it:
flesh and blood,
frail, once hearty,
who wore it at the last weary, needy.

How easy to reify you,
O woman of the name Catherine,
to forget the thread of your own life and story
within the fabric of Mercy.
O timeless woman it is easy to forget
how much of your own time you were,
subject to its limitations and ignorances,
as well as its promise,
its constraints as well as its freedoms.

Although not seamless, this garment
speaks of the pain and failing
of one who had sat by so many beds,
held the hand of so many dying.
Could she have dreamed, this one small woman
that beyond her own final confinement
would spring not death
but the birth and burgeoning of her line?

Catherine's Room – the Cup and Saucer

Did it bring you comfort this china,
the little cup worn at the rim and
translucent as the shell of an egg,
reminding you of Coolock days,
the warm liquid soothing and refreshing?
Did you read the leaves all those years ago
and know your life would end
here in quite another place?

Of life filled
life emptied.
Of call given
and fulfilled.
Of encouragement and conviviality,
bonds of kinship
and gesture of gracious hospitality.
Taking the cup of your life,
drinking the sweet-bitter draught that was yours.

the chapel

Silence seems the right word for the place,
sitting in the deep silence.
And then old words come,
ancient words sung and spoken,
one voice and together:
Salve
Ave
Magnificat
Suscipe

Over and over in the simplicity of chant,
enhanced by the rich resonances of a vaulted ceiling,
the ancient voices sing.
So many women's voices singing women's songs
and in the coloured glass high up to either side
with the expected heroes, the great heroines of the faith:
Brigid of Kildare, Catherine of Siena, Teresa of Avila:
all mission-contemplatives,
activists and women of spirit,
a feisty feminine trio.
Who made these choices for the windows,
what were they meant to inspire
in those who looked at them?
Admit me to their company
that I may sit with them in attendance to your Word.
Bring me to that ancient silence,
lead me to that ancient song.

The Five Punt Note*

You have entered the Dublin vernacular:
not just the nun at the Herbert St. bus stop,
but there with the wordsmiths Yeats and Joyce
and the great feminine winsome Ireland
Cathleen ni Houlihan watermark.
Winsome enough yourself there,
an icon of grace in a world of mixed fortune,
the old religion on the new.

You who knew the power of the greatest Word
have become daily currency
for petrol and paper,
ordinary commodities of fish and bread
in shop and farmyard,
as well as grime and vice,
where the prostitutes linger not far from here,
down by the banks of the Grand Canal.

If only this money were mercy,
and the religion of commerce
made a daily currency of compassion and kindness
by which all would profit,
but especially the uninfluential,
the unaffluent and the desperate.

But sadly and gladly
Mercy is a currency minted solely
in the heart,
from the heart given
and from the heart received.

Since this was written the introduction of the Euro has superseded the Irish currency, so sadly Catherine is no longer legal tender!

the callaghan room

Praise God for you
William and Catherine Callaghan,
who led that other Catherine to many years
of bedside reading
inscribing on her heart the dynamic word,
the word finding her a ready memory,
the word falling into rich soil,
buried for later in the earth of daily devotion;
the word smoored in the hearth,
banked down for the great fire of tomorrow.

Thank you Callaghans
for your gracious silences,
for your hospitable kindnesses,
for your need of her care,
a barren couple
whose legacy was life through her life,
gift which became her gift,
a small mercy made large by
the kindnesses of that one house Coolock,
whose inner light
yet radiates God's love.

She must have loved you to have brought with her
so much that reminded of life with you,
so much more than mere things,
however fine,
imbued with memory and meaning,
tokens of fondness and blessing for her.

Intercede for us, Catherine and William,
that our mercy
may always be informed by the inner light
of right silences,
the strength of right conviction,
the belief in each one's dignity.

The Deed of Agreement

In the polite parlance, common usage of the day,
you are designated 'Spinster'
on this deed of agreement for your ambitious
building plan.
An image of making in this lovely spiral stairwell,
a confluence of feminine images.

Expectant the spinner spins
preparing her dowry as in days of old,
the word now derisive meant first the maiden who spun,
making the household linen for her future home
in anticipation of her life partner.

She has a secret this spinster McAuley:
a gold ring of betrothal
a thin but pure thread of gold.
What is her dowry
but what she has to give of her very self
and what has been given to her to share from this house?
'Maiden yet a mother'
a maid not old,
yet never to be worldly wife.

From you I reclaim the power of the spinner/spinster:
a word no longer mean or fraught with lost opportunity.
You show the spinner's way and calling,
for in another deed of agreement
entered into with the Master Builder,

although you remain the eternal spinster,
you are bride of Christ,
busy at the wheel,
spinning,
stretching the fine fleece of God's grace
into wool for garments of Mercy.

tomb

If life is a voyage then this
tomb is a ship,
like Gallarus oratory in the west,
a stone boat sure on eternal seas.

Angels guard the one born on Michaelmas,
the feast of the great angel.
'For time and eternity' it says,
echoing your prayer,

A declaration for a lifetime,
a surrender of soul to the kairos of the spirit,
a mutual possession,
a mutual pledge,
a surrender to the waves of God.

God was praised in you,
Mercy made in you,
lives helped and healed by you,
the times informed and shaped by you.

God be praised for you
and mercy made in this time, and for eternity,
in the name and the spirit
you have left us.
For time and eternity.

the illuminations

Could one look about the place and not make
for you, Clare Augustine Moore,
one small work of tribute and admiration,
not merely for your art,
which glows yet with vigour and flourish,
you who executed in colour and letter
the journeying Word
and the new Mercy way,
one artist in a long line
who bent over words for the sake of the Word.

Thank God too for you yourself, first Mercy artist,
Thank God that you remained true to your true calling
and that Catherine knew that you too were at home here,
since pragmatism sometimes needs art
to lend light to the spirit.

Sculpture: The Circle of Mercy*

Catch the No.10 Bus along Baggot St.
and alight at the Herbert St. stop.

You will come
face to face with a veiled woman, a cailleach,
the wise old woman of Irish mythology.
Well, not quite face to face, since she is a towering,
larger than life figure.

She is not alone, this wise one, protector of the land.
Here is a configuration of the feminine,
a womanly trinity: mother, child and nun.

One hand is outstretched.
Is it a gesture of giving or of begging,
a welcome or a movement of farewell?

The outstretched foot from one angle looks almost dainty,
like a dancer preparing to leap,
but move to the side and you will see
that that foot is like an anchor,
or the root of some great sturdy tree,
the leg massive.
The weight of the figure rests on that leg,
a complete contrast to the hand suspended
delicately in air like a bird's wing.
That leg gives balance to the unseen hand behind,
firmly gentle at the mother's back:

to embrace, to propel, to steady/to guide/to protect/
to comfort/to reassure/to strengthen/to encourage/to
love.

They stand outside the house;
like St. Brigid who was born on the threshold,
that zone of inclusion or exclusion,
the way in which is the way out,
liminal, marginal, marvellous.

She owns the house who ordered it built,
yet she is not entirely free to be its mistress,
pressures and priests and notions of the proper obtrude.
On the street perhaps she is freer to greet and to seek,
to welcome and console.

This a circle that is not a circle,
a circle in the making,
a circle at the waiting,
awaiting a response from the onlooker,
each onlooker the missing arc that completes,
makes the circle mercy.

---

* The work of sculptor Michael Burke, erected in 1994, and titled Circle of Mercy, stands outside the front door of Mercy International Centre.

welcome

The last time I was there
It rained all day in Dublin,
and nothing soft about it.
I scurried along Baggot St
dodging sodden umbrellas,
and as I turned into the entrance way of
64a Baggot St,
there she was, her hand outstretched,
an accidental holy water stoup.
I smiled my flesh and blood smile
At the bronze woman,
And tucked my fingers around hers
dipping into the water and gripping the metal
as a touchstone
a code
a meeting
a pledge
baptism
again
anew.

it claims us

Somehow it claims us, this rectangle of land,
insisting its kinship.
Its felicity is not in its exterior,
the unadorned bland.
Its face to the street is unremarkable
but for the bronze figures who greet you,
and the recent modest roundel asserting a city's interest.
And yet it draws us, the house,
we belong to it.
The house beckons us
to listen to the murmuring of its beams
to await its revelations
through floor, stone and wood
and the light infused, rainwept glass.
By its lintels and spaces we are defined,
our DNA is in the dust fallen between floorboards.
We may think we come as observers,
but in truth we are observed-
observed with a kind scrutiny,
measured by mercy,
measured for mercy.
Why is this house sacred?
Because here God's grace met human disposition,
here God's eloquence met human effort
and sparks flew,
fire found a purpose.
And we, we are kindred, kindled, flame.

Proof of being here

This is a place, a space,
of earth and air and light,
hidden spring and flame,
this is a shelter and haven
a cradle and crucible,
a house and a turbine
where it is entirely apt
to want to leave the footprint
of your soul,
to pledge a thumbprint
you will recognise on return,
to incise laden graffiti
in some imagined stone within the walls
or hidden atop a lintel of aged wood-
the proof of being here
the pride of learning from it
the joy of knowing that you
are confirmed here
in your mercy, and that memory
will bless you at each recall.
What secret word
do you entrust to this place,
this space,
this house
until you return for real
or in the spirit's vivid dream-
what is the word you give,
the word you receive?

the long line

It is said of Brigid's successors at Kildare
that they kept her fire alight
unabating
a thousand years or thereabouts.
I think of those
who have lived in this house,
who kept its memory crisp,
its spirit thriving-
this fine old special house-
the named and the unnamed,
the saints and the strugglers,
the clear-headed and the muddlers,
of those who lived long lives here,
growing old with the building,
their bones creaking through Dublin winters
on bare floorboards before central heating,
of those who died here young and stricken,
of diseases we don't see often today, if ever,
and of those noblest who having long loved it
left it so that others from all the world
could meet here the spirit of a generous heart.

Give thanks for those who kept the home fires burning,
minding the house,
keepers of the hearth.

venerable*

Venerable is prismatic,
a word that refracts into
august age and solemnity, due honour, the extraordinary.

In some ways it puts at a distance the one it esteems,
renders her superhuman,
when in reality she was fully human
because fully given to the Light that is God,
totally Catherine in her own skin,
being what she was meant to be,
uniquely Catherine in her own spirit,
attuned to God as friend.

She knew the power of laughter
before endorphins had a name,
she took on whatever landed by sad circumstance-
becoming adoptive mother, ready ingatherer;
she received gladly the fortuitous-
hefty inheritance, likeminded companions;
she shared life, did not covet it closely to herself –
animate, she said, and animate she did-
a word that leaps beyond itself.
She advised the exquisite care called tenderness,
this woman who encouraged rather than censured,
who liberated despite the constraints
of culture and church.

Extraordinary she *was,* but only because
she lived the ordinary,
seeing the colours of God always,
the rainbow of need and response,
help and heal, pray and be present.

Yes, we venerate her as exemplar,
standing with reverence by the holy space she fills-
a human being, a woman,
who found herself a friend of God, Catherine of Dublin.

Such a spirit shines on, whatever title it is given.
We cannot emulate her uniqueness; we must live our own.
We do our best to live in our way the mercy she gleaned,
drawn to the friendship- with her, with the great God,
catching the colours for our day.
Catherine- such a spirit shines on:
it helps and heals, prays and is present.
Venerable is prismatic.
It refracts into the true colours of
Sancta, Naomh, Santa, Santu, Saint.

*(Celebrating 25 years since Catherine McAuley was declared Venerable.)

mercy is*

Mercy is a woman of indeterminate age
and unremarkable appearance.
She is not fussy about the company she keeps,
and tends to be full of excuses for her friends,
having seen life from their angle.

Her heart, like her pockets, is capacious.
She has a voice rich in tender understanding
But is at her best in silence
when she sits alongside
the grief-stricken and the guilty
and their sorrow seeps into her soul.

Curiously, she sees herself reflected
in the eyes of both murderer and victim,
so sits not in judgement but companionably.
She is a subtle teacher.

She makes strong cups of tea, cup after cup.
Her hands are worn by work
but eagerly sought by the dying.

Her feet are calloused from long roads
trudged with refugee and beggar.
She is an endurer of all horrors.

Mercy has a face wrinkled by kindness
and worn by the cost of living,

but even in hovels she has been given to laughter
and awareness of simple pleasures.

She has a store of lore and wisdom
but is never heard to complain
that she's heard any story
a hundred times before,
believing each teller to be
entitled to a hearing as if to the one and only.

Mercy is a lady comfortable to be with-
the safest and soundest-
blessed in her being
with the indisputable reality
that she is true daughter,
in manner and in mind,
of the maker of the universe.

*the feminine metaphor is a metaphor not a gender prescription and is not intended to exclude. Permission is given to adapt the pronouns according to circumstances if required.

blessing for the road

May the God of mercy continue to lead us and inspire us.

May the spirit of Catherine be a light
and a joy for the road.

May the compassion of Jesus be our guide
and our measure.

In the name of the Trinity of love:
Creator, Word and Spirit.
Now and always,
Amen.

Day

Mercy rests in thankfulness,
wakes in compassion,
works with fidelity, tenderly,
sleeps with the door ajar.

monosyllabic

Mercy works with monosyllables mostly-
A yes, a no, a you and we.
Not terse but tender
is her plain speaking brevity.
She listens, she tends,
a Martha-like Mary:
a touch, a wordless sigh,
the cup, the quiet care.
When sermons
and lectures
and advice
and chat
have no place,
when answers
and solutions and neat endings flee,
in the company of grief and shock
and bone-weary sadness,
the monosyllables of Mercy hold sway.

UTTER

If we utter aloud the word *mercy*,
standing, each of us, by an open window
anywhere we are in the world,
then the word *mercy* will carry on the soundwaves
onwards and unceasing,
through the air of the wounded world.
And maybe, when it takes flight
into deed and kindness, justice and effort,
it will effect a healing, a hope and a blessing.
It may call the homeless home,
it may coax to hope the betrayed and broken,
it may ease the burdened earth.
Listen for it, the repeated word *mercy*, on this Mercy day,
Listen for its neighbourly dialects and global idiom.
Imagine those who, like you, are saying it aloud,
and those who need to hear it, today- the word- mercy.
One word, one deed of justice, one kind effort at a time.

Creator God, sustainer of life,
Jesus, our companion Word,
Spirit, who, like the air, inspires,
give us the simple daring this day
to say and to be Mercy.

mercy full

Merciful make my heart
O God
Mercy full as Yours,
with space for need and time to pause.
Merciful make my heart.

meeting

May you meet mercy each day:
in the light of your own heart,
at the hands of your loved ones,
in the eyes of the stranger and the needy.
And if by chance you do not at first meet it,
then search your heart for it,
listen patiently for word of it,
and it will tap you on the shoulder,
a quiet surprise,
a small gesture
the tender look,
given and received
in the encounters of your day.

need and knowing

May your own need and knowing of mercy
lead you to its need and its knowing in others.

before sleep

Reckon each night
in the quiet dark
the mercy-blessing of your day:
its giving and its taking,
its abundance and its subtlety,
its recognition at the
meeting-place of spirit.
Be in the gladness of your heart.

Prayer for a Mercy Day

Into the mercy of Jesus your child,
into the mercy which is the wondrous womb of God,
rich with creative blood,
into the mercy which insists "alive is the Spirit,
alive and awake and waiting,"
Into this mercy-
O girl of Nazareth,
O woman of Calvary,
O matriarch of Pentecost-
Into this mercy
coax our need,
release our enslavements,
lead our fears,
invite our dreams.

Woman of mercy-
who knew within your womb
the first limberings
of the one who *is* mercy-
teach and lead and free
and find
with us and for us
the place where sit the ones who weep
and starve and ail and mourn and
do not own more than an inkling of future.

Let us be with them and for them
a word, a way,
and a flashpoint of that mercy.
O great woman,
O mother,
our sister in Jesus:
Mary,
this, today,
for this time,
we pray.

garden*

All gardens are sacred, but this over and above,
its grass fed from the bones of goodness,
a green enclave for reverence and reverie,
where the spirits murmur
into the silence and the distant bustle of Dublin days.
The primary sound of Ireland is not city but water,
as it trickles, flows, pours and lashes;
here and now it soothes
rocks already smoothed by Ireland's great waters,
carried here to keep this mercy water company.
Ancient rocks from perhaps the mighty Shannon
that wends through eleven counties,
no hard borders in its way;
stones are they from the Slaney, the Moy, the Liffey,
the Foyle, the Barrow, the Lee,
a stone's throw from the spirit-soaked stones of
Clonmacnoise and Cashel, Lady's Island and Kells,
rocks that were old when Brigid and Patrick
walked on them,
rocks of sandstone, granite, and limestone
revealing quartz-gleam in the light,
layers of time and pressure, patterns of grace and stress,
the upheaval of volcano, the sediment of sandstone
compressed with tiny ancient creatures of the oceans,
and the water-permeable, welcoming grace
of the limestone:
the play and power of water engaged
with the endurance and amenability of stone.

Very much at rights with its origins all this,
but called too by the crafted orb
to consider the wider earth,
the broader waters of the world-
the orb that holds tendrils and leaves and butterflies,
gaps to see the sky and feel the air-
there- put your hands tenderly through the world-
hints of creatures supple and sinuous, but no snakes,
that's certain,
a globe that furls and unfurls the spirals of life
and today's tune enticed with that trace of treble clef,
as it sends the water flowing past names and memories
from many lands laden with mercy stories,
all enhanced by the delicate tiled colour of flowers,
mercy made one art to another, one stone to another,
one person to another,
past to present and on it flows.
And lest we forget,
turn and see, she who began it all
sits here at last, the bronzed woman,
giving and taking the air, inspiring still.
Go sit with her and listen.

Commissioned by Mercy International Centre for the rededication of the garden at Baggot St, 2019.

knowing

'In knowing my Mercy
you will learn little by little
to make my mercy,
and
to make it known, my mercy,
to be it in flesh and to meet it in flesh.'

God's Favourite Hue

If love is the essence and measure of God
mercy must be God's favourite hue,
a subtle shade
which tells of need and blessing
of pain and waiting
of love greater than grief
of simple joys and tenderness,
of sharing the colours of life.

Litany of Mercy

Creator God- Maker and Source of Mercy -
all praise to You.
Jesus - exemplar and champion of Mercy -
all praise to You.
Spirit- artist and animator of Mercy -
all praise to You.

Out of the profound silence of Your Presence we murmur the words of Mercy:

- ❖ Rahamim: the womb love - *inscribe it on our hearts.*
- ❖ Hesed: the loving kindness - *inscribe it on our hearts.*
- ❖ Eleos: the healing oil - *inscribe it on our hearts..*
- ❖ the words of tenderness and empathy - *inscribe it on our hearts.*
- ❖ the words of tolerance and forgiveness - *inscribe it on our hearts.*
- ❖ the words of justice and faithfulness - *inscribe it on our hearts.*

In the encounters of the life of Jesus we find our Mercy meaning:

- ❖ the woman with the alabaster jar- *may we meet as Jesus met.*
- ❖ the rich young man - *may we meet as Jesus met.*
- ❖ the little girl brought to life - *may we meet as Jesus met.*
- ❖ the three at Bethany - *may we meet as Jesus met.*
- ❖ the lepers, the outcasts, the lost - *may we meet as Jesus met.*

In the imagination of Jesus we find our Mercy inspiration:

- ❖ the one sheep who went missing - *may we do as Jesus told it.*
- ❖ the son who was welcomed home - *may we do as Jesus told it.*
- ❖ the vineyard workers, late and early - *may we do as Jesus told it.*
- ❖ the treasure buried in the field - *may we do as Jesus told it.*
- ❖ the only one who stopped to help - *may we do as Jesus told it.*

In the life of our forebears we recognise Mercy:

- ❖ for Mary of Nazareth and Calvary - *we thank You.*
- ❖ for Catherine McAuley, woman of Dublin - *we thank You.*
- ❖ for our founders and pioneers, the near and the far - *we thank You.*
- ❖ for our holy ones and wisdom figures - *we thank You.*
- ❖ for the heroic and the humble - *we thank You.*

With all Your creation we share our life in Mercy:

- ❖ the feather and the fur - *we respect and cherish.*
- ❖ the waterway and the breeze - *we respect and cherish.*
- ❖ the rock and the leaf - *we respect and cherish.*
- ❖ the fish and the star - *we respect and cherish.*
- ❖ the flame and the stalk - *we respect and cherish.*

The colour of mercy - *we celebrate.*
the shape of mercy - *we celebrate.*
the mystery of mercy - *we celebrate.*
the arenas of mercy - *we celebrate.*

The unfinished chapters - *we pledge mercy.*
the unmet need - *we pledge mercy.*
the violence, the horror - *we pledge mercy.*
the urgent immensities - *we pledge mercy.*
the cries, the silences, the aches and injuries - *we pledge mercy.*

In Your name, with Your help, by Your hand.
In the large days and ordinary ways,
alone and together, we are people for Mercy.
Mercy calls us - *Mercy calls us.*
Mercy guides us - *Mercy calls us.*
Mercy sustains us - *Mercy calls us.*

Amen.

FRIENDS

God of the immense universe,
God of each human heart,
We thank You and we praise You.

We are people from many parts of the world -
diverse of tongue, talent and place -
who pray together as
friends of mercy and
friends for mercy.

We are united by a spirit and a story
born in a house in Dublin,
now spread to the outer reaches of the earth
and the inner recesses of the heart.

As friends in mercy,
united in that spirit and story,
we commit ourselves to
preserving the best of the past,
fostering the best of the present,
and shaping the best for the future.

We pray in the name of Jesus,
with the help of Our Lady of Mercy,
 and inspired by the life of Catherine McAuley.

Amen.

be

Mercy be the name;
Mercy be the path;
Mercy at the heart.
Ever, ever. Amen.

www.ingramcontent.com/pod-product-compliance
Lightning Source LLC
Chambersburg PA
CBHW071904290426
44110CB00013B/1273